The Complete
Jewish Guide to
Britain and Ireland

Also by Toni L. Kamins

The Complete Jewish Guide to France

A TRAVEL GUIDE

The Complete Jewish Guide to Britain and Ireland

Toni L. Kamins

 St. Martin's Griffin ≈ New York

In Memoriam
Klara Markovitz

ז״ל

פייגע בילה בת רפאל שמואל וחנה

THE COMPLETE JEWISH GUIDE TO BRITAIN AND IRELAND. Copyright © 2001 by
Toni L. Kamins. All rights reserved. Printed in the United States of America. No
part of this book may be used or reproduced in any manner whatsoever without written permission except in the case of brief quotations embodied in critical articles or reviews. For information, address St. Martin's Press, 175 Fifth
Avenue, New York, N.Y. 10010.

www.stmartins.com

Maps by David Lindroth

Library of Congress Cataloging-in-Publication Data

Kamins, Toni.
    The complete Jewish guide to Britain and Ireland / Toni L. Kamins.—
1st ed.
        p.   cm.
    Includes bibliographical references (p. 135) and index.
    ISBN 0-312-24448-7
    1. Great Britain—Guidebooks.   2. Jews—Monuments—Great Britain—
Guidebooks.   3. Jews—Travel—Great Britain—Guidebooks.   4. Jews—
Monuments—Ireland—Guidebooks.   5. Jews—Travel—Ireland—
Guidebooks.   6. Judaism—Great Britain—History.   7. Jews—Great
Britain—History.   8. Judaism—Ireland—History.   9. Jews—Ireland—
History.   10. Ireland—Guidebooks.   I. Title.

DA650.K25   2001
914.04'86—dc21

                                                            2001041618

First Edition: September 2001

10   9   8   7   6   5   4   3   2   1

Contents

Acknowledgments

My work on this book was a wonderful journey of discovery and rediscovery. The time I spent in England on research allowed me to rediscover a country and people I had long ago come to love and respect. When I was a child, my father's stories about his experiences as a soldier stationed in England during World War II compelled me to read about the country and to travel there myself as soon as I was old enough.

Through my work in this book, I was able to discover the history and culture of the Jews of England—something I already knew about but was grateful to have the chance to examine in greater depth.

There were a number of people who assisted me on this project and I am very grateful to all of them. They include: Dr. Sharman Kadish of the Survey of the Jewish Built Heritage; Rickie Burman of the Jewish Museum; Evelyn Friedlander of the Hidden Legacy Foundation; Susie Symes and Philip Black of the immigrant museum being established at the former Princelet Street Synagogue; Charles Tucker of the office of England's Chief Rabbi; Tony Kushner of the University of Southhampton; Sam Gruber of the International Survey of Jewish Monuments; and Jeff Bloomfield. I am especially grateful to David Jacobs of Reform Synagogues of Great Britain for his informational assistance, but also for some of the wonderful photographs contained herein, and to his father Leonard Jacobs, and to the late Roger Cowen.

I am also grateful to New York City's Writers Room, where this book was really born, for providing me with a very hard-to-come-by commodity in New York—a quiet place to work, free from distraction—and to the Byrdcliffe Colony for the Arts in Woodstock, New York, which gave me a residency during the crucial first few months of this project.

My thanks to Andrew Miller and Greg Cohn, former editors at St. Martin's Press, who first gave the green light to the project; to Kristen Macnamara and Joanna Jacobs, who saw the project through to completion, patiently I might add; and to my agent, Carolyn Krupp of IMG Literary, who has at least as much patience.

Thanks to the monthly dinner group: Dan Hurley, Norman Schreiber, Erica Manfred, Minda Zetlin, Marion Betancourt, Florence Isaacs, Linda Konner, Joan Iaconnetti, and Janet Bailey.

Special thanks go to Charles Ruas, whose encouragement was ever present on two continents, and to Adrian Leeds, for her limitless supply of ideas.

As always, my family was around to provide support while they eagerly awaited publication. Thanks to my parents, Walter and Judith Kamins; and to my sisters, brothers-in-law, nieces, and nephews: Erica, Nick, and Conor Farrell; Jennifer, Richard, Marissa, Tamara, and Jake Bullock; and Dana and Jeff Jacobs.

I find that even as a writer I am at a loss to find the words that express adequately my appreciation to my husband, Harold Itzkowitz. Without his love, support, and valuable criticism this, along with many other things, would not have been possible.

Travel Basics

Getting There

BRITISH AIRWAYS HAS the most daily nonstop flights to London and other cities from major U.S. cities, including ten daily flights from both JFK and Newark to London. Tel: 800 247-9297 (800/AIRWAYS). Information can also be found at their website http://www.british-airways.com. BA also flies to Scotland from the U.S. and to Ireland via London. **Aer Lingus** flies to Dublin from New York, Newark, Boston, Chicago, Los Angeles, and Baltimore–Washington. Tel: 800/IRISHAIR; online http://www.airlingus.com.

Getting Around

TRAINS

Intercity travel in England is fairly easy by train, and using London as a hub makes it convenient to travel to other parts of the country via London's train stations. Unless you have a lot of time, you might consider flying instead to far-off cities like

Manchester (5 hours from London by train) or to Scotland. For train information before you leave home, contact:

- **Rail Europe** is the U.S. representative for all the European railroads and can sell you tickets to anywhere you want to go on the continent, including the Eurostar that operates between London and Paris or Brussels. Tel: 888 382-7245; hours: M–F 9 AM–9 PM. Online go to http://www.raileurope.com/us. In addition to selling Eurail passes, Europasses, single tickets, and other travel services, they offer various rail passes just for France. This is also the site to get your BritRail passes for travel within the UK—Eurail passes are not valid in great Britain.

- For information about railway timetables and the like for travel in England, go to http://www.railtrack.co.uk/travel online.

CARS

Unless you're familiar with driving on the left, you might do better with some other mode of transportation. A car in London will be a definite liability, but if you do want to drive, consider renting a car only for that portion of the trip that will take you outside the capital. Rentals are available through:

- **AutoEurope** (888 223-5555; http://www.autoeurope.com)
- **Hertz** (800 654-3001; http://www.hertz.com)
- **Avis** (800 230-4898; http://www.avis.com)

Getting to Ireland from England

*D*UBLIN IS A short flight from London and the trip can easily be done in a weekend. **British Airways** (800/AIRWAYS) flies from London, and the Ireland-based Ryan Air has inexpensive flights from the London City Airport (from London 0541/569-569; online http://www.ryanair.com).

Getting to Scotland from England

*B*OTH BRITISH AIRWAYS (800/AIRWAYS; http://www.british-airways.com) and British Midland Airways (800 788-0555; http://www.flybmi.com) have nonstop flights from London to Edinburgh and Glasgow. British Airways also flies nonstop to Inverness, as does Ryan Air.

Getting to Wales from England

*T*HERE IS TRAIN service from London's Paddington Station to Cardiff, Swansea, and other cities in Wales. Contact http://www.rail.co.uk or Rail Europe at 877 456-RAIL.

Getting to Paris from London

GONE ARE THE days of the boat train across the English Channel and gone are the days of hauling out to the airport to get from London to Paris. Eurostar is the way to go. With several daily trains in both directions, the 3-hour trip couldn't be easier—the Chunnel portion is only 22 minutes. There are several ways to buy tickets. My favorite is via Eurostar's website http://www.eurostar.co.uk. I then pick up my ticket at Waterloo International just before I have to board the train. You can also purchase tickets for pickup or delivery in London or Paris on the French Railway website http://www.sncf.com (there's an English language version too), or through Rail Europe 877 456-RAIL or http://www.raileurope.com. Kosher meals are available with advance notice in first and premium classes. Inquire when making your reservations.

Getting Around London

DON'T EVEN THINK about renting a car here. Traffic is just awful, parking is impossible, and if you don't know the city well—trust me—you don't need a car. If you're starting your trip in London, wait to rent a car when you are ready to visit another part of the country. And remember, the controls are on the opposite side of the car and driving is on the left side of the road, passing on the right. It is not as easy as it looks. If you're not used to it, I don't recommend it.

London can be a confusing city. It is vast and the streets have no pattern. So your trip to London will be made far easier if you get a copy of *London A–Z.* Its index lists every street and alley and then refers you to coordinates on one of its highly detailed maps of different areas of town. It also includes an Underground map. It's just indispensable—even Londoners carry it around. It's available at newspaper/magazine kiosks, at most bookstores, in newspaper and magazine shops, and at online stores such as Amazon (http://www.amazon.com).

THE UNDERGROUND A.K.A. THE TUBE

Though Londoners complain about it, and it is often the subject of derision and controversy in the press, the London subway system is the best way to get around town. It's fast, safe, and it goes virtually everywhere.

If you're going to be in London for more than a few days, you'll want to buy a pass that allows you unlimited Underground access and includes the bus. It's called the **Travel Card.** You'll need a passport-type photo, available from machines at most Underground stops. Prices vary according to the number of zones you want included, but if you will be primarily in central London, a two-zone pass should suffice. Keep in mind that London has "subways" too, but those are underground passages across streets and have nothing to do with mass transit.

Telephones

$\mathcal{E}$NGLAND HAS BEEN revamping its phone system and many internal numbers and prefixes have been changed and will continue to change.

The country code for England, Scotland, and Wales when

calling from outside the country is **44,** Ireland's is **353,** and Northern Ireland's is **028.**

London's new code is **020** and all London phone numbers begin with either a 7 or an 8 following that code. Within London it isn't necessary to dial 020. To call London from outside the country, drop the first 0.

For directory assistance in London, dial **142;** for the rest of England, **192.**

Money

*A*TM MACHINES (also called cashpoints) are omnipresent in all but the smallest towns and traveler's checks are really a thing of the past when you're coming to Britain. Use the ATMs just as you do at home. Just be sure that your PIN is four digits (if your PIN is longer, have your bank change it); and if you only know your PIN in letters, memorize it in its numerical form—ATM keypads are numbers only. One thing more to note: at an ATM at home you have a choice of withdrawing cash from your checking or saving account, outside the country you won't have that choice. The funds will be withdrawn from whichever account is the primary account—usually it's checking. So make sure there is enough money in that account to cover your withdrawals.

Major international credit cards (Visa, MasterCard, American Express) are widely accepted. As a precaution against theft, though (pickpocketing is a big problem in London), you might want to carry some money in travelers checks and make sure to keep them and your credit card account numbers, as well as the stolen card telephone numbers, in a separate place. Traveler's checks can be exchanged at banks where you will get better terms than at currency exchanges.

Hotels

*N*OTE: THESE ARE all personal recommendations. The hotels listed below are in the first-class category and rooms cost $300 per night and up, though you may be able to do a bit better with one of the many package deals all these hotels offer. London hotels are not cheap—even in the moderately priced and budget ranges. All are well maintained, have private bath, minibar, telephone, television (with cable and CNN), in-room safe-deposit box, hair dryer, elevator, are open year round, and accept all major credit cards. They also have 24-hour room service, concierge, laundry service, and other amenities.

LONDON

The Millennium Mayfair. 44 Grosvenor Sq., Mayfair, London W1K 2HP. Tel: 020-7629-9400; Fax: 020-7629-7736. http://www.stay.with-us.com; E-mail: reservations.mayfair@mill-cop.com. Tube: Bond Street.

Overlooking the sedate Grosvenor Square in the heart of Mayfair, and adjacent to the U.S. Embassy, this well-appointed and convenient hotel has good-size rooms and top-notch service. Recently refurbished, it also has many business amenities such as in-room Internet access and a full business center.

Red Carnation Hotels is a small chain of boutique hotels in some of London's best and most convenient neighborhoods. Go to http://www.redcarnationhotels.com online.

The Chesterfield Mayfair. 35 Charles Street, Mayfair, London W1X 8LX. Tel: 020-7491-2622; Fax: 020-7491-4793.
E-mail: reservations@chesterfield.redcarnationhotels.com.
Tube: Green Park.

> Located in the heart of Mayfair, this small, intimate boutique hotel is a quick walk from the Green Park tube station and just two blocks from Berkeley Square. Nearby is terrific shopping—Oxford, Bond, and Regent Streets, and Kensington. You can even walk to the theater if you're feeling energetic. As is the case with many hotels in London, rooms tend to be on the small side, but the Chesterfield's are more than adequate. Service is generally good, but can be spotty at times. The staff is responsive so don't be afraid to speak up.

The Montague on the Gardens. 15 Montague Street, Bloomsbury, London WC1B 5BJ. Tel: 020-7637-1001; Fax: 020-7637-2516.
E-mail: reservations@montague.redcarnationhotels.com.
Tube: Russell Square.

> If the British Museum is your destination, this quaint townhouse hotel is the place for you—it's just across the street. With Soho, Covent Garden, and lots of shopping nearby, the Montague makes a convenient headquarters for your London stay. Rooms are small but adequate, and the bilevel suites are very charming (bedroom on one level, sitting area on another). The staff is eager to please.

The Rubens. 39 Buckingham Palace Road, London,
SW1W OPS. Tel: 020-7834-6600;
Fax: 020-7233-6037.
E-mail: reservations@rubens.redcarnationhotels.com.
Tube: Victoria.

Situated directly across from Buckingham Palace, the
Rubens offers convenience coupled with every amenity. The
cozy, comfortable rooms are beautifully decorated and
appointed and the staff will see to it that you are made
welcome and happy.

Number 41. 41 Buckingham Palace Road, London,
SW1W OPS. Tel: 020-7300-0041;
Fax: 020-7300-0141.
E-mail: reservations@41club.redcarnationhotels.com.
Tube: Victoria.

Next-door to the Rubens and accessible via a private
entrance from its lobby, Number 41 is a new breed of
London hotel—it's all-inclusive. Though pricey, your room
rate includes full English breakfast, a light buffet served all
day and evening, cocktail and bar service, canapés and
snacks every evening, laundry, dry cleaning and all valet
services, traditional afternoon tea, fully stocked minibar, free
local calls and calls within the UK, mobile phone and laptop
rentals, and butler's pantry for late-night refreshments.
There is also in-room fax and a selection of CDs and movie
DVDs. Many rooms have live flame fireplaces. The sixteen
rooms and four suites are smallish, but they are skillfully
decorated and very well appointed. My favorite? The bilevel
suite with a king-size bed underneath a glass skylight.
Number 41 has some terrific weekend packages that include
theater tickets.

The Milestone. Kensington Court, London, W8 5DL.
Tel: 020-7917-1000; Fax: 020-7917-1010.
E-mail: reservations@milestone.redcarnationhotels.com.
Tube: High Street Kensington.

The view from the front of the Milestone is of Kensington
Palace (home of the late Princess Di) and its gardens. The
interior is no less opulent. The rooms are individually
decorated, some along thematic lines—the hunt room, the
jungle room, and a panoply of whimsy that will make your
stay even more fantastic. There are also wonderful private
apartments.

How to Use This Book

Structure

THE FIRST CHAPTER of the *Complete Jewish Guide to Britain and Ireland* is designed to give you an historical overview of the history of the Jewish people in Britain even before you get to the travel part. I've done this so that you will better understand the historical background of the sights that you will see. Each city chapter contains a shorter, but more specific history of the individual community. Having already read the introductory chapter, you will then be able to put the local information into a broader context and emerge with as full a picture as possible (within the limits of an historical travel guide) of the historical and social fabric in which the buildings, museums, synagogues, cemeteries, neighborhoods, and even churches you visit exist.

Some chapters contain little of specifically Jewish interest and are very short—only one or two pages. Keep in mind that after the general expulsion of Jews from England, Jews did not settle many towns and cities again. Most of those places had small communities to begin with so little, if anything, remains. That is not to say that there isn't anything worth seeing. But the usual tourist sights are, for the most part, beyond the scope of this book.

Resource Sections

*A*T THE END of each city chapter, you will find lists of
resources. Many of these are aimed at observant Jewish travelers who require kosher food, places to pray, and other
necessities such as "mikvaot" (ritual baths). But they also contain lists of Jewish bookstores and other establishments that the
nonobservant and non-Jewish traveler should feel free to visit.
Even if you don't keep kosher, a good Jewish meal might be just
what you're looking for—a little chicken soup for the soul, as it
were. Some places have no kosher food available at all, and in
some places it may only be available at the synagogue or Jewish
community center. In those cases, a call to the synagogue might
result in an invitation to someone's home for a meal, especially
on Shabbat.

I have also provided a section on "Keeping Kosher in
Britain"—specific information on the various authorities that
supervise kosher food. For those of you who eat fish in
nonkosher restaurants, I have also included a list of kosher fish,
featuring some that might be unfamiliar to travelers not from
Great Britain or Ireland.

Cemeteries

*T*HERE ARE SEVERAL old Jewish cemeteries in
Britain—some date back to the seventeenth century.
Some are still in use and others have not been used in many
years. In most cases, the cemeteries are locked and gated and
access can be a problem. Frequently, they have no specific
address and require an appointment with the caretaker or

somebody from the local Jewish community to visit. In every instance, I have listed a contact number for the cemetery or the name or phone number of someone from the Jewish community who can help you. This is not a formal process, and it's best to call a few days ahead to see if you can reach someone. Be aware that many of the older headstones are severely weather-beaten and difficult, if not impossible, to read.

Access to Jewish Sights

*N*OT ALL OF Britain's Jewish sights are accessible to the public and some buildings have been converted to other uses and are now in private hands. Britain has come somewhat late to the task of Jewish historical preservation and often the Jewish establishment has to be convinced of the worthiness of these endeavors. Were it not for the efforts of a small and very dedicated group of people, there would be far less to see.

Keeping Kosher

THE MAIN SUPERVISING authorities are the Beth Din, Kedassia, the Federation Kashrus Board, and the Sephardi Kashrus Authority. The Beth Din is run by United Synagogue, Kedassia by the Union of Orthodox Hebrew Congregations, Federation by the Federation of Synagogues, an Orthodox group, and the Sephardi Kashrus Authority by the Sephardic Synagogues.

As you might have guessed, most kosher restaurants, bakeries, prepared food shops, etc. are in Jewish neighborhoods, so if you do keep kosher and you are not staying in a Jewish neighborhood, you will need to keep this in mind when planning your meals. In London, for example, there are only a few kosher options in the areas with the most tourist attractions. Golders Green, the large Jewish suburb with lots of kosher food, is a good forty minutes on the tube. Outside of the cities with large Jewish populations it's advisable to contact the local synagogue or one of the other Jewish organizations listed to learn about the availability of kosher food.

Packaged items are clearly marked by whichever organization supervises kashrut, and restaurants and other food stores display a certificate. There may be unmarked packaged items or unmarked foods such as ice cream that are in fact kosher, and you can call the Beth Din for a list of those.

Telephone numbers:

London Beth Din: Tel: 020-8343-6255 or 020-8343-6270

Kedassia: Tel: 020-8800-6833

Federation Kashrus Board: Tel: 020-8202-2263

Sephardi Kashrus Authority: Tel: 020-7289-2573 or
020-7203-2228

Manchester Beth Din: Tel: 161-740-9711

Glasgow Beth Din: Tel: 141-637-5171

Introduction

LIKE MOST AMERICANS, American Jews come from someplace else. It may have been our parents, grandparents, great-grandparents, or ancestors before them, but at some point our families lived in some other country. The vast majority of our families come from one or more European countries, and it is for that reason that this series of *Complete Jewish Travel Guides* begins with the countries that make up both Western and Eastern Europe.

To many American Jews, European Jewish history starts and ends with the Holocaust—the Shoah. That series of events that took place in several countries between 1939 and 1945 during World War II, nearly has become one amorphous occurance in some minds. But there is so much more to European Jewish history than that. As you will discover in each country covered in this series, Jews have lived in Europe for some two thousand years—long before Adolf Hitler and the Nazi Party. And they continue to live and thrive there today, despite them.

Visiting Jewish communities around the world is an age-old Jewish tradition. Throughout the centuries, travelers and emissaries have chronicled the Jewish settlements of their day and have visited the synagogues, cemeteries, and other landmarks of their coreligionists. Though there was, in centuries past, a very strong religious component in the work of those emissaries, interest in the legacy of Jews in various parts of the world has never been exclusively religious. It has also provided a means of forming a cultural connection between Jews from one place with Jews in another. And it can be a bridge between past, present, and future.

From the fall of Jerusalem in 70 C.E. until the founding of the modern State of Israel in 1948, the Jewish people were without an official country. Persecution, murder, high taxes, and ghettos were all a part of life for Jews in Europe. But wherever they lived during the great Diaspora, they left their traditions in the form of synagogues, schools, monuments, neighborhoods, and cultural institutions. It is through those that today's traveler, veteran or first-timer, can become better acquainted with the vibrant Jewish communities that rose from the ashes and thus learn about their neighborhoods, institutions, and centuries-old culture.

So come along with me on a journey of rediscovery. I promise you won't be disappointed. Your comments are welcome. Please contact me in care of the publisher or at www.complete jewishguides.com.

CHAPTER ONE

The History of Jews in England

JEWS CAME TO England fairly late compared to their arrival in continental Europe. Whereas Jews already had communities in places such as France, Germany, Italy, Spain, and Portugal, centuries before the end of the first millennium, they didn't get to England until 1066. In that year, a small group of Jewish financiers came from northern France along with William the Conqueror and his armies from Normandy. The majority were French, although some of the Jews in that group had lived in Germany, Italy, and Spain.

Some one hundred years later, Jews had settlements throughout England. London, the most vital of England's Jewish communities, was the site of the country's only Jewish cemetery. Other important communities could be found in Bristol,

Winchester, Oxford, York, Norwich, and Lincoln. While Jews lived under Norman rule, they enjoyed a high degree of freedom and had many rights. But early in the twelfth century, public and governmental anti-Jewish sentiment began to emerge.

England's first known blood libel (see below) occurred in Norwich in the East Midlands in 1144. Other such incidents took place in Gloucester in 1168, Bury St. Edmonds in 1181, Bristol between 1181 and 1183, and Winchester in 1192. But by the end of the thirteenth century, such calumny had disappeared from England.

The Blood Libel

Employed throughout history as a pretext for the murder and persecution of Jews, the blood libel or ritual murder alleges that Jews hunt and kill Christians (usually children) and use their blood in the baking of Passover matzoh and for other religious rituals. It has its origins in an absurd notion that Jews hate people in general, and Christians and Christianity in particular. In addition, it takes some of its power from the superstition that Jews are not human and have to ingest potions so that they may appear human.

The myth of the ritualistic use of human blood by Jews goes back to ancient times when pagans, who used human blood in sacrifices (a practice forbidden to Jews), misunderstood the Jewish ritual of removing all blood from meat by salting.

The superstition evolved into a myth perpetuated by the Greek empire at a time when there was considerable tension between Jews and the Greek governors of large parts of what is now the Middle East. Along with Christianity, the myths made their way into Europe, and by the Middle Ages they had become firmly rooted.

*Europe's first clear case of blood libel against Jews was in
England in 1144. But it quickly spread throughout Europe,
where the Middle Ages and early modern times saw numerous trials and massacres of Jews as a result. An integral part
of European lore, the blood libel was used well into the twentieth century, most notably in Czarist Russia, by the Nazis,
and in the mid-twentieth century by the Soviet Union in its
anti-Israel propaganda.*

Throughout the twelfth century, Jews in England were subject to a variety of special taxes and fines. Criminal charges
against individual Jews, whether true or false, often resulted in a
fine for the entire community. One such fine occurred in 1130,
when the Jews of London had to pay a total of £2,000 because
one Jew was charged with murder.

Despite such financial hardships, England's Jews prospered
and the taxes on their wealth and property became a significant
source of the kingdom's revenue. Financiers such as Aaron of
Lincoln, whose estate became the property of the Crown when
he died, were responsible for the construction of buildings
throughout the realm.

But high taxes were not the only difficulties Jews had to
endure. As it had on the European continent, the zeal of the
Crusaders to liberate the Holy Land from non-Christian influ-
ences took a toll in Jewish lives. Many London Jews were murdered during a riot that followed the coronation of Richard I in
1189. Small and large communities fell victim, in one way or
another, to riots. The Jews of Dunstable converted to Christianity, the Jews of Lynn were massacred, and the Jews of Norwich,
site of the first blood libel some years earlier, met the same fate
as those of Lynn. In York, in March 1190, the entire Jewish community decided to commit suicide rather than face a massacre at
the hands of an angry mob. It should be noted here that when

England had to pay a ransom for the release of Richard I from captivity, the Jewish share was three times that of the rest of the population.

It is difficult to know for sure which Jewish crime, so to speak, was the greater—the rejection of Christianity or the fact that so many Christian noblemen and commoners owed money to Jewish moneylenders. Murder and mayhem against the Jewish community were never enough; the perpetrators were intent on reneging on their legitimate debts by destroying all records. But this didn't just prevent Jews from getting repaid, it also prevented the Crown from collecting taxes on Jewish income. The negative impact on the income of the Crown was profound and Richard I was forced to take action. In 1194, he created a special office, staffed by both Jews and Christians, for storing duplicate copies of transactions negotiated with Jews. This Ordinance of the Jewry thus protected debt records in case the originals were destroyed. Even the original draft of the Magna Carta contained a stipulation that limited Jewish collection of debts from an estate of someone who had died.

The Ordinance of the Jewry eventually became an Exchequer of the Jews, a national office charged with overseeing the regional ordinances. In addition, the Crown established the office of the Presbyter Judaeorum, an expert on Jewish issues whose job was to advise the Crown in those financial and related matters.

Money Lending

According to the Torah (the basic document of Jewish law), Jews are forbidden to loan money at interest to other Jews, and there are a number of interpretations of the Torah's wording that go so far as to eschew the taking of interest from anyone. Likewise, the Roman Catholic Church was opposed to the charging of interest in any form. Nonetheless, when merchants, governments, and individuals were in need of funds and they hãd none of their own, they borrowed it from the wealthy who loaned it at interest.

Jews were not the only people in the money-lending business—this type of commerce crossed religious lines despite the Church's stand against it. Money was borrowed from priests, merchants, landowners, and even Popes. In much of Europe, Italian merchants, such as the Lombards, the Medici, and the Caursini, competed with Jews in the lending of money at interest. But as Jewish interest rates were regulated by the various governments, their terms were far better.

In the Middle Ages, money lending became a critical source of Jewish income because Jews were excluded from virtually every other occupation. In some cases they were specifically limited to earning a living by lending money, and interest rates that Jews could charge were strictly regulated. Indeed, interest charged by non-Jewish parties was much higher. But all that regulation begs the question: Just who did run the money-lending business, Jews or the governments that regulated them; and whose income was dependent on the tax income derived from them?

Exorbitant taxes continued throughout the reigns of King John and King Henry III. But it was during the time of Henry III that things went quickly from bad to worse.

In 1222, the (Church) Council of Oxford set the stage for more difficult times to come when it promulgated its own version of the Fourth Lateran Council's Anti-Jewish laws. That council, which was convened in Rome in 1215 by Pope Innocent III, had a dramatic effect on the daily lives of Jews throughout Europe because it mandated numerous restrictions on their daily life and their means of earning a living. A contemporary account of Jewish life in England from 1066 to 1738 lists the following:

- No Jew shall remain in England unless he performs some sort of service for the King. As soon as possible after birth, any Jew, male or female, shall serve in some manner;

- There shall be no synagogues in England except those that were in existence at the time of King John;

- Jews shall worship in their synagogues in a subdued tone, in such a way that Christians will not be able to hear them;

- No Christian woman shall suckle or nurse any Jewish child, and no Christian man or woman shall be the servant of any Jewish man or woman, nor eat or stay with them in their home;

- No Jewish man or woman shall eat or buy meat during Lent;

- No Jew shall denigrate the Christian religion or dispute about it in public;

- No Jew shall have carnal relations with any Christian woman, nor any Christian man with a Jewess;

- Every Jew shall display his badge of identification *[in England the badge depicted the tablets of the Ten Commandments]*;

- No Jew shall in any way hinder any other Jew who wishes to convert to Christianity;

- No Jew shall be allowed in any town without special licence *[sic]* from the King, except those towns where Jews customarily reside.[1]

It doesn't take any special historical insight to see that hundreds of years later, when the Germans were formulating the Nuremberg Laws—the segregative laws in Nazi Germany that preceded the Shoah (Holocaust)—they had a solid foundation on which to base them.

Between 1232 and 1255, synagogues in England were confiscated and ritual murder accusations increased. After 1253, Jews could no longer live just anywhere in England—they could only live in places where there was already an existing community.

Little Saint Hugh

In the spring of 1255, sometime around Passover, the body of a young boy, Hugh, was found in the well of Lincoln's Jewish quarter. As the well was near the house of a Jew named Copin, he was questioned and tortured and was alleged to have admitted killing the boy to obtain his blood for use in Jewish ceremonies. Copin was executed and nearly one hundred Jews were tried in London as accomplices. Eighteen were executed.

Looked upon as a saint, but never actually beatified by the Roman Catholic Church, Little Hugh was credited with the performance of miracles. His tomb, under Lincoln's cathedral, was an elaborate one that became a destination for pilgrims up until the Reformation.

The so-called martyrdom of Little Hugh is mentioned in Chaucer's "The Prioress's Tale" and was also the subject of ballads in England and France.

The Barons' War (1263–67), a civil war in which a baronial council tried to reform both local and national government, opened the Jewish community to further attack because the Jews were believed to be the Crown's partners in its fiscally oppressive policies. Cities all over England were pillaged and Jewish property was destroyed.

By 1272, when Edward I became King of England, Jewish wealth had been whittled down to nothing and the money-lending business had been taken over by bankers from elsewhere in Europe. Because Jews were no longer a great source of revenue for the Crown, King Edward issued the Statutum de Judaismo in 1275, designed to give Jews the right to engage in other forms of commerce on a trial basis. Although legally Jews could now practice trade, they were prohibited entry into the Guild Merchant, and for all practical purposes that meant trade would remain closed to them. So Jews continued to practice money lending in secret and others resorted to clipping coins—taking pieces of metal from coins circulated by the treasury. This was a serious crime and in 1278 many Jews were arrested and hanged for it—even many who had committed no crime at all.

Frustrated that the Statutum de Judaismo had failed to achieve its goal, and beset by difficult economic and political problems, Edward I expelled the Jews from England on July 18, 1290. The relatively small Jewish community of approximately 4,000 persons moved to France, Germany, and Flanders. Jews would not live in England again until the seventeenth century. This period has become known historically as the Expulsion. Though there was no organized community during this time, it is believed that a group of a few Conversos did live in England. Conversos, also referred to by the derogatory Marranos, were Spanish and Portuguese Jews who pretended to convert to Christianity while they practiced Judaism in secret. Among them were Roderigo Lopez, Queen Elizabeth I's physician, who was beheaded based on the accusation that he was trying to poison her, and Hector Nunez, who advised the Crown in its dealings with Spain. But in 1609 this group of Conversos was also expelled.

Another small community of secret Jews entered the country in 1630 and they would later form the foundation of the first Resettlement community. It's likely this group of secret Jews had at least one secret synagogue—probably in someone's house in what is now the City of London.

The Resettlement

A COMBINATION OF factors led to the Resettlement—some that were political and some that were even mystical.

England in the seventeenth century was a country beset by political and religious strife. In the end a civil war between the supporters of King Charles I and the supporters of the Parliamentarian military and political leader Oliver Cromwell (1599–1658) erupted. Against this chaotic social and political backdrop, which was contributing to changes in religious and political belief, was a feeling among some groups that Jews should be readmitted to England. Among these groups were the Baptists and the Puritans—the same Puritans who were the first English colonists in America.

The Puritans, who believed in the basic precepts of the Bible, particularly the Old Testament—hence the name Puritans—were drawn to the Jews because of their connection to it. Such favorable feelings toward Jews did not endear the Puritans to the decidedly anti-Jewish establishment Church of England. Other Christians who favored a literal interpretation of the Old Testament and differed with mainstream Christianity about the nature of God were persecuted. Such groups were said to hold Judaistic opinions.

The English civil war ended with the execution of King Charles I in January 1649 and ushered in the period known as the Commonwealth—Cromwell was the virtual dictator. The new constitution drawn afterward, the Agreement of the People, would set the stage for Jewish resettlement. One of the first official petitions came from a group of Baptists who requested that Jews be granted the same sort of settlement and trading privileges that they enjoyed in the Netherlands. Others in England were convinced that England's troubles were the result of its maltreatment of the Jews. But there was still considerable opposition to having non-Christians living in England and an amended version of the Agreement of the People mandated that religious freedom be permitted only for those who believed in "Jesus Christ."

Eventually it was not religious tolerance or the desire to convert Jews to Christianity or Jewish financial acumen that would convince Oliver Cromwell that his position in favor of readmission was correct. It was his belief that Jews could play an important role in his dreams of Empire and he was willing to overlook their idiosyncratic religious practices in order to achieve his goals.[2]

The mystical component came via the beliefs of one Manasseh ben Israel, a leader in the Amsterdam Jewish community. Born in Madeira and baptized Manoel Dias Soeiro, ben Israel was the son of a Converso who fled a Lisbon auto-da-fé (literally act of faith—the Inquisition ceremony that reconciled penitents, often by burning them at the stake) and settled in Amsterdam. Ben Israel's father, Gaspar, renamed his sons Ephraim and Manasseh and gave himself the name Joseph ben Israel. Many Conversos maintained vestiges of Jewish practice in secret for many generations. Some, like Joseph ben Israel, became Jews outwardly again once they were safely away from the clutches of the Inquisition. Amsterdam, with its religious tolerance and liberal atmosphere (certainly for the times) was such a safe place.

As a Jew in Amsterdam, Manasseh grew up practicing his faith and became a respected scholar, well educated in Jewish texts and Jewish theology. He earned the respect of his fellow

Jews as well as Christians because of his broad knowledge of the Bible. He wrote extensively on Biblical subjects and founded Amsterdam's first Hebrew press (1626). One of his books, in Latin, was *The Hope of Israel*. In it he wrote about Jewish communities throughout the known world and noted that there were no Jews in England. Now the medieval word for England is Angle-Terre—as it is in modern French and Angle Terre means corner of the earth. Ben Israel believed, as did most Jews of his day (and to this day), that one of the pre-conditions of the coming of the Messiah is the dispersion of the Jewish people Kezeh ha-Aretz—the Hebrew for "end of the earth." As Angle-Terre was devoid of Jews, ben Israel felt that resettlement there would hasten the coming of the Messiah. He dedicated the English edition of *The Hope of Israel* to the English parliament in the hope that they would take up his cause.

At the same time as Manasseh ben Israel was writing and publishing in Amsterdam, Baptists in England were attempting to have Jews readmitted to England. There was a genuine feeling among this group that religious tolerance was needed. In addition, the Baptist leaders pointed out that Jews could not be converted to Christianity if they were not around. Many supported bringing Jews back with the proviso that they make no attempt to convert Christians to Judaism. That was not likely to be a problem, as Jewish tradition does not seek out the convert.

After several years of negotiations by ben Israel's surrogates aimed at readmission, ben Israel himself arrived in England in 1655 with a plea to Oliver Cromwell, the Lord Protector. Later that year a group of judges met at London's Whitehall to consider the matter. Though many were in favor of readmission, many others, merchants and theologians, were not and Cromwell adjourned the conference after four sessions. At the same time, the Conversos already living in England petitioned for a cemetery and after many months the petition was granted. Though not formally admitted back to England, it was obvious that the government was willing to look the other way and the Jewish community existed de facto if not totally de jure. Despite an indefinite legal status, the Jews of London were able to practice Judaism openly.

A revealing look at a contemporary Christian view of synagogue practice comes to us via a 1662 letter from John Greenhalgh to his friend Thomas Crompton. Greenhalgh visited the synagogue in London's Creechurch Lane and described what he saw in great detail. In addition, it provides Jews today with a thought-provoking glimpse of our own past. Not surprisingly, observant Jewish readers will find that the scene looks very much like the present.

> When Saturday came I rose very early, the place being far from my lodging; and in a private corner of the City, with much ado, following my directions, I found it [*the synagogue*] at the point of nine o'clock, and was let come in at the first door, but there being no Englishman but myself . . . I was first a little abashed to venture alone amongst all them Jews . . . I went in and sate me down amongst them . . . what a strange, uncouth, foreign, and to me barbarous sight was there, I could have wished Thomas that you had then sate next me, for I saw no living soul, but all covered, hooded, guized, veiled Jews, and my own plain bare self amongst them.
>
> Every man had a large white vest, covering, or veil cast over the high crown of his hat, which from thence hung down on all sides, covering the whole hat, the shoulders, arms, sides and back to the girdle place, nothing to be seen but a little of the face; this [*I was told*] was their ancient garb, used in Divine Worship in their Synagogues in Jerusalem and in all the Holy Land before the destruction of their City: and though to me at first, it made altogether a strange and barbarous

show, yet me thought it had in its kind, I know not how, a face and aspect of venerable antiquity. Their veils were all pure white, made of taffeta or silk, though some few were of stuff coarser than silk . . .

They do not suffer the Women to come into the same room or into the sight of the men; but on the one side of the Synagogue there is a low, long, and narrow latticed window, through which the women sitting in the next room do hear. . . .

At the east end of the Synagogue standeth a closet like a very high cupboard, which they call the Ark, covered below with one large hanging of blue silk; its upper half covered with several drawing curtains of blue silk; in it are the Books of the Law kept. . . .

Then the Priest arose and some of the chief Jews with him, and they went with a grave slow pace up the Synagogue, to fetch the Law of Moses, and when they came to the Ark wherein it was kept, the priest drew the curtain, and opening the double door of it, the Law appeared, then the whole assembly stood up and bowed down just toward it, and the priest and those chief ones with him, stood singing a song to it a little while. The Law was written on two great rolls of very broad parchment. Then there arose one out of the assembly and came unto the priest, making low reverence: when the priest asked aloud whether he desired to hear the Law read, who saying "yes" the priest bade him pray then, and he looked upon his Hebrew Service Book which he had in his hand, and read over a short prayer very fast; then the priest read a few lines of the Law with a loud voice in a thundering barbarous tone, as fast as his tongue could run, for a form only; then asked the man whether he had heard the Law, who saying "yes" he bade him give thanks then, and he read a short prayer out of his book as before: so, bowing himself to the Law and the Priest, he went to his place, and another came, and did in like manner until five or six had thus heard the Law read to them; which they count a special piece of honour to them. . . .

This forenoon service continued about three hours, from nine to twelve, which being ended, they all put off their veils, and each man wrapping his veil up, went and put it and his Hebrew Book into his box, and locking it departed.[3]

King Charles II, who as Prince of Wales lived in exile in France at the time of the civil war and the execution of his father (Charles I), was restored to the throne of England in 1660. Although he was a Roman Catholic King in a country of Protestants and favored religious tolerance, he was not of a mind to change the situation of the Jews in England, though there was considerable pressure for him to do so, but finally, after several years of persecution, the Jewish community was granted a promise of the freedom to worship in 1673 and again in 1685. Such protection was to continue throughout the Stuart monarchies (James II, Queen Mary II, Queen Anne). In addition, during this time there were no special Jewish taxes. In 1698, the Act for Suppressing Blasphemy acknowledged Judaism in England, albeit indirectly.

Freed from most of the restrictions and heavy taxes that encumbered Jews in other parts of Europe, the Jews of England prospered. As England's empire grew and expanded, the community gained importance in the all-important field of finance. The most successful Jews of the community were engaged in trade and brokerage—among them were Samson Gideon and Joseph Salvador, who were advisors to the government.

Some restrictions did remain, however—a Jewish family was obligated to support a child even if that child converted to Christianity, and the number of Jewish trade brokers in London was limited to twelve. But apart from that, the only real unhappiness was a relative isolation from the rest of the Jewish world—at the time, the only other community in the British Isles was in Dublin. Soon, though, immigration from Amsterdam, Spain, and Portugal increased the numbers of the Jewish community, and Jews settled elsewhere in the empire—North Africa, New York, India, and the West Indian islands of Jamaica and Barbados.

As the community grew and moved into the relative mainstream of London and English society, they found that they needed a larger synagogue to accommodate their numbers—the one they were using, located in Creechurch Lane in what is now the City of London, was too small. In 1701 a new one was erected nearby on the small street known as Bevis Marks (*see* chapter 2).

We know from history that wherever a Jewish community has found refuge and relative social and political safety, other Jews soon follow. It was no different in England. In the late-seventeenth century, the existing Sephardic group of London was augmented by a group of Ashkenazim (Jews of Eastern and Central European origin and customs), first from Amsterdam and Hamburg and later from other parts of Germany and Eastern Europe. A formal community was founded in 1690, and as always seems to happen in every Jewish community, a split developed resulting in the formation of several new ones. So by 1761, there were three Ashkenazi communities in London.

Beginning in the middle of the eighteenth century, small Jewish settlements began to crop up in other English cities as a result of the small-time Ashkenazi peddlers who roamed the length and breadth of the country. They left London and its surrounding area and moved to the areas around cities such as Manchester, Liverpool, Birmingham, Portsmouth, and other places. During the week they sold their wares in the countryside and in small towns, and then they returned to the cities for the Sabbath.

There was at the same time a marked difference not only in the culture of the two Jewish groups, the Sephardim and the Ashkenazim, but also in their economic status. The Sephardim were, for the most part, financiers and business brokers. Though they were all immigrants at one point or another, the Sephardim regarded themselves as socially superior to their newer immigrant coreligionists.

Though Jews had indeed come a long way in England and were doing well, free of most of the former restrictions, they were by no means universally accepted, and there were still a few legal, social, and economic impediments to full equality. So in 1753, when the Jewish Naturalization Bill, known as the Jew Bill, was introduced into Parliament, there was such extreme opposition that the government withdrew it—though it did not precipitate violence as it once might have. The bill would have provided for Jews born outside of the country to obtain the same legal rights granted their native-born children.

But the anti-Jewish sentiment was such that it drew the normally divided Ashkenazim and Sephardim together in common cause and laid the foundation for an umbrella organization that would become the Board of Deputies of British Jews—an organization that exists to this day.

The nineteenth century saw some great changes for Jews in Europe. A movement for Jewish emancipation and civil rights in France, begun in the last quarter of the eighteenth century, finally came to fruition at the beginning of the nineteenth. In granting French citizenship rights to France's Jews, Napoleon, eager to subsume Jewish loyalties to the French state in the interest of empire abroad and France at home, completed the process initiated by such French philosophers as Charles-Louis de Montesquieu (the *Persian Letters*; the *Spirit of the Laws*) and prominent Jews in France such as Herz Cerf Berr. The French movement provided an impetus for native-born Jews in England to push for the same thing.

Not coincidentally, a renewed movement for Jewish emancipation came close on the heels of one for Catholic rights. Though the House of Commons passed the Jewish Emancipation Bill in 1833, it was rejected several times by the House of Lords despite strong support from people such as historian Thomas Babington Macaulay, Robert Grant, and the Duke of Sussex, son of King George III. In 1846, the Religious Opinions Relief Bill chipped away at still more restrictions on full Jewish participation. In the intervening years, Jews were appointed to a number of high municipal offices, but it would be another twelve years before a Jew could take a seat in the House of Commons.

It was an odd state of affairs. Lionel de Rothschild was elected to the House of Commons by his London constituency again and again beginning in 1847. But because the House of Lords opposed legislation permitting a non-Christian to take the required oath, he could not actually serve those who elected him. Finally, in 1858, after years of wrangling, a settlement was reached that permitted each house of Parliament to make its own rules regarding the oath. While Commons made provisions for non-Christians, the House of Lords adamantly opposed any change. It still would be nearly thirty years more before a Jew could be elevated to the peerage and take a seat in the House of Lords. That distinction went to Nathaniel de Rothschild, the son of Lionel. One could argue, however, that the first Jewish peer was really Benjamin Disraeli, Lord Beaconsfield. His father, a member of London's Bevis Marks Synagogue, had converted Disraeli to Christianity when he was still a child. But though he never practiced Judaism, Disraeli made no secret of his birth and was always sympathetic to Jewish affairs. According to Jewish law, a Jew is still a Jew regardless of his or her conversion to another faith.

The remaining restrictions notwithstanding, during the mid-nineteenth century, England had a Jewish solicitor general,

Sir George Jessel, and London had a Jewish Lord Mayor, Sir David Salomons.

The Rothschilds

The Rothschilds have been prominent in English finance, arts, letters, and philanthropy since the middle of the nineteenth century, and for some two hundred years the House of Rothschild, which has branches in Europe's financial capitals, has played a major role in the economic history of Europe and indeed the world.

The family came originally from Germany and it takes its name from the red shield that hung in front of the Frankfurt house of Isaac Elhanan, the grandson of a man named Uri, the first recorded Rothschild, who died around 1500. The family continued to use the name though they no longer lived in the house.

Some one hundred and sixty years after the death of Isaac Elhanan, Mayer Amschel Rothschild was born in 1744. At the age of twenty-five, Mayer Amschel became a court agent to William IX of Hesse-Kassel, with whom he had done business in antique coins for some years. He gradually built up substantial financial holdings and created a successful business.

Nathan Mayer, the son of Mayer Amschel, left Germany to settle in Manchester in 1797. A dealer in textiles, he left for London in 1803 and married. His business acumen soon resulted in his becoming a key member of London's stock exchange and he became a valuable aide to the government when he and his brother, James, the head of the French branch of the family, acted as financers of Wellington's army in Spain. The financial resources of the family saw the British and allied governments through the last battles of the Napoleonic wars. In the aftermath of the war, the Rothschilds were instrumental in providing loans and bonds for reconstruction.

Lionel Nathan Rothschild (1808–79), the son of Nathan Mayer, was in the forefront of the Jewish emancipation movement in England. Elected to Parliament in 1847 as a Liberal, he could not actually take his seat until after the passage of the Jews' Disabilities Bill in 1856. Under his stewardship, the Rothschild bank loaned money to the British government that funded aid to Ireland during the famine, the army during the Crimean War, and the purchase of the Suez Canal.

Along with his wife Charlotte (the daughter of his uncle, Carl Mayer von Rothschild of Naples, and therefore Lionel's first cousin), Lionel was very active in philanthropic work in England's Jewish community and provided funds that established Jewish institutions outside of England. Their children, Nathaniel Mayer (1840–1915), Alfred (1842–1918), Leopold (1845–1917), Annie (1844–1926), and Constance (1843–1931) were similarly active.

Nathaniel, known as Natty, succeeded his father as head of the family business and also as the leader of the English Jewish community. He has the distinction of being the first Jewish peer and the first Rothschild to receive a visit in his own home by Queen Victoria. As the only Jewish member of the Royal Commission on Aliens, Nathaniel went against the popular wisdom that wanted to restrict immigration to England.

Though Nathaniel was opposed to Zionism, his son, Baron Lionel Walter (1868–1937), was not. It was this second Rothschild to whom the British foreign secretary, Lord Balfour, wrote the letter that constituted the Balfour Declaration (see page 25).

Other members of the family have included Lionel Nathan (1882–1942), the son of Leopold (1845–1917), the brother of the first Lord Rothschild. Lionel Nathan became *president of the United Synagogue. Others were his brother Anthony Gustav (1887–1961), and Edmund Leopold (1916–), the nephew of Baron Lionel Walter. The third Baron Rothschild, Nathaniel Mayer Victor (1910–90) was a renowned biologist.*

The interwar period saw the rise of other large banking firms and the power of the Rothschild bank began to ebb. A special target of the Nazi government, which put a high premium on getting hold of Rothschild assets, the family had the foresight to get their holdings to safety in neutral countries before the Germans got their hands on it. As a new economy began to emerge following World War II, the Rothschilds followed suit and sought out new types of investments.

Today the Rothschilds continue to be a major philanthropic force all over the world and are still active in politics. As is the case in many Jewish families, Rothschilds have begun to marry non-Jews and, as a result, have taken a reduced role in the British Jewish community's affairs.

Social and economic conditions for Jews in Eastern Europe created the huge wave of immigration of the late-nineteenth and early-twentieth centuries. Though most Americans know that hundreds of thousands came to New York City and the rest of the United States, less well known is the fact that large numbers also found their way to England. Immigration from Eastern Europe, mainly from Poland and Russia, increased the Jewish population of England from 65,000 to 300,000 between 1880 and 1914. As the Eastern European Jewish immigration changed the nature of the existing American Jewish community, it also changed the nature of the community in England. Where the more established English Jews were fairly well assimilated, increasingly less observant, largely middle class, and living away from the old urban centers they had settled generations before, the new immigrants were Yiddish speaking, poor, and Orthodox.

Settling in congested, working-poor neighborhoods in London's East End, Glasgow, and the manufacturing cities of Manchester, Leeds, and Liverpool, the new immigrants took up the small clothing trades and tailoring, along with cabinetmaking.

Of course the existence of Jewish communities of even small size engendered a whole host of institutions—newspapers in Yiddish and Hebrew, and various communal and fraternal groups. And as was common in most growing Jewish communities, small groups of Jews each founded their own small synagogue, or Chevra.

Establishment Jewry went to great lengths to assimilate the new immigrants into English Jewish society, and English society in general, by providing classes in the English language and creating institutions aimed at fostering social assimilation, such as London's Jews' Free School. In addition, youth clubs such as the Jewish Lads' Brigade added to the social education of immigrant children. And there was very little opposition to assimilation by the immigrants—in fact, they so welcomed it that the whole process was hugely successful. Even the most observant Jews among the newcomers found little fault with the synagogues as the religious service followed the traditions to which they were accustomed, even if life itself was less strictly Orthodox than it had been in the old country. There were, of course, small groups that didn't really care about blending in—some Orthodox, the secularists, and those whose politics leaned far to the left—but, for the most part, English Jewry were culturally English as they entered the twentieth century. But for a growing, vehement anti-immigrant and anti-Jewish backlash, the picture would have looked quite rosy.

During the late-nineteenth and early-twentieth centuries, England had few restrictions on immigration. The public, though, along with many trade unions, feared a wage depression because of the influx of new immigrants and a loss of jobs for native Englishmen. This was particularly true in the textile trades, and hard economic times only exacerbated this fear. The immigrants' need for housing in the same lower-class neighborhoods as poor native-born English led to concerns about increases in rents in an already-tight housing market. Above all, many English feared foreigners, and foreign Jews in particular, and worried that their English Christian country would be overrun by these strangers. The Jewish community worried too. The existing organizations, which had been set up to integrate new Jewish immigrants, could be overwhelmed by the sheer numbers of immigrants, which would defeat the purpose for which they had been established. Even in the face of horrendous anti-Jewish persecution in Russia, some Jewish leaders went so far as to discourage immigration to England because they believed that the persecution was temporary. However by 1903 and 1904, when the gruesome news of government-sanctioned pogroms in Russian cities such as Kishinev, Smela, Gomel, Rovno, and Aleksandriya surfaced, the Jewish resistance to immigration ceased.

Meanwhile, accusations that immigrants were deliberately driving down wages and causing rent increases became increasingly widespread. But on several occasions, when the government investigated, the charges were always found to be without merit. That notwithstanding, the investigations culminated in the establishment, in 1903, of the Royal Commission on Aliens, which proceeded to make several recommendations designed to ease the current difficult conditions and allay public fear. Then, in 1905, the government placed restrictions on immigration in the form of the Aliens Act. However, because the act accommodated those seeking asylum from religious persecution, the practical effect on immigration was inconsequential.

Some of the anti-Jewish backlash came from the literary set. The Catholic writer Hillaire Belloc, in works such as his 1922 *The Jews*, promulgated the belief that Jews, along with Protestants, were civilization's enemies; G. K. Chesterton and Rudyard

Kipling attacked what they perceived to be Jewish influence in the halls of power and money, and D. H. Lawrence and Graham Greene demonstrated their animosity for Jews in many of their works. This literary anti-Semitism was set against the social world of the late Victorians and the Edwardians in which Jews such as the Sassoons, the Rothschilds, and Baron de Hirsch were found in the circle of the Prince of Wales (the future Edward VII) and in the chambers of Parliament as Conservative MPs, though most Jews in politics were members of the Liberal Party.

By the mid-nineteenth century, English Jewry had begun to feel secure and at home in England, and they began to expand their organizational activities to promote the security of Jewish communities outside England—especially in Muslim countries. In those undertakings they also formed alliances with Jewish organizations in other countries—the Anglo-Jewish Association, for example, was established to work with France's Alliance Israelite Universelle in reaction to the anti-Jewish incidents that followed the Franco-Prussian War in 1871. Sir Moses Montefiore was a sort of delegate on behalf of establishment Jewry in general and English Jewry in particular, and he lent his considerable influence, which included the support of the British government, to a number of philanthropic and community causes.

The Damascus Affair

In 1840, Jews in Damascus, Syria, were accused of ritual murder by the local Christian Arabs after the disappearance of a Capuchin monk and his servant. Over one hundred Jewish men were sent to prison and tortured, including some prominent local Jews. The French government, backers of Mehmet Ali, the Egyptian ruler of Syria, supported the charges, so the powerless Jews of Damascus sought help from their British and French brethren. Sir Moses Montefiore and France's Adolphe Crémieux, vice president of the Consistoire

Centrale, the official representatives of the French Jewish
community came to their aid. Though the Damascus Jews
were released, the fallout had far-reaching effects on the Jews
of France. Jews, mainly in Alsace, were attacked and their
houses and property were damaged. Eventually, the army had
to be called in to restore order.

In addition to reaching out to Jewish communities outside
of England, any number of organizations were formed at home
to better serve English Jewry. Most of these new enterprises were
based in London. London was still the center of English Jewry,
though to be sure, there were already communities in the
provincial industrial cities. Before too long after industrializa-
tion, the cities of Manchester, Birmingham, Leeds, and Brad-
ford, along with cities in Scotland, Ireland, and Wales, would see
the growth of significant Jewish communities, and the Jews of
some of those cities would come to dominate the nascent ready-
to-wear clothing industry.

One of the most significant enterprises was the *Jewish
Chronicle*, which had been founded in 1841. Now the oldest
continuously published Jewish publication in the world, it was
the first permanent English Jewish newspaper. England's first
seminary for training rabbis came into existence in 1855 as Jews'
College in London, and the Jewish Board of Guardians (now the
Jewish Welfare Board) was founded in 1859 to serve the poor.

One of England's dominant Jewish religious groups was and
still is the United Synagogue. Begun as a quasi-umbrella group of
London's Ashkenazi synagogues in the early-nineteenth century,
an 1870 act of Parliament helped establish it as a more formal
entity. It remains today a very influential Jewish organization.

World War I

J EWISH IMMIGRATION TO England ceased in 1914 with the start of the First World War, and anti-German sentiment was the order of the day. It was so intense that the royal family, whose name was the Germanic Battenberg, decided to change it to the more English-sounding Mountbatten. Today they are known as the Windsors and the Windsor-Mountbattens.

At the time, the Jewish community found itself in an interesting predicament. The demand for uniforms created by the war was responsible for a huge increase in ready-to-wear clothing production—a Jewish business. But because most Jews worked in industries that were not really vital to the war effort, they were drafted into military service in far greater numbers than the rest of the population. That is not to say that they did not go willingly, and Jewish soldiers distinguished themselves in battle in WWI. Some 50,000 Jews were under arms for England, and Jewish casualties numbered more than 10,000. Of those who served, 1,596 were decorated—six with the Victoria Cross, the nation's highest military award. There were even some special Jewish battalions of the Royal Fusiliers who fought in Palestine and helped to defeat the Ottoman Turks.[4]

The Balfour Declaration and British Zionism

T HE HISTORIC DECLARATION was in reality a letter (dated November 2, 1917) from Lord Arthur James Balfour, the British Foreign Secretary, to Baron Lionel Rothschild, a leader of the British Jewish community. The contents declared British support for a Jewish national home in Palestine. But the outward simplicity of the document belied the international political machinations that had motivated it. It would become the hope of a long-persecuted Jewish people, the bane of a budding Arab nationalism, and a bloody tether binding Great Britain to her shrinking empire in ways she could not anticipate at the time. As it turned out, the Balfour Declaration was one of the most significant developments of World War I.

By 1917, the World War I allies were making plans for control of the ruins of Ottoman Turkey's empire—the postwar Middle East. Great Britain and France jockeyed for hegemony of lands that had been ruled by the Ottomans for over four hundred years. Not coincidentally, the Ottoman defeat signaled a dramatic increase in the efforts by the young World Zionist Organization to secure support for Jewish historical claims to a national home in Palestine. Zionist leaders such as Chaim Weizman (who would later be Israel's first president) and Nahum Sokolow worked tirelessly to secure multinational support for a Jewish state.

England's first Zionist movement was Hovevei Zion (Lovers of Zion) in 1887; its principal leaders were engineer and author Elim d'Avigdor and the Indian-born Colonel Albert Goldsmid. Early Zionist groups such as Hovevei Zion predated the beginning of political Zionism founded by Theodor Herzl in the wake of France's Dreyfus Affair in 1897. Alfred Dreyfus, the only Jewish officer on the French army's general staff, was tried and found guilty of treason based on forged documents and perjured testimony concocted by his anti-Jewish colleagues. Dreyfus' public degradation in Paris in 1894, and the anti-Jewish demonstrations it stimulated, motivated Herzl to develop his own ideas for a modern Jewish homeland—Zionism. Their emphasis was less on securing a state than it was on solving the living situation of Jews in countries where they were clearly pariahs. As a result, they concentrated on encouraging Jews from Eastern Europe to move to Palestine in the wake of the pogroms of the 1880s and after. It was for this reason that the majority of Hovevei Zion's members were to be found among recent immigrants to England, though many members of the English Jewish community supported it. But British Jewry didn't really climb on board the Zionist bandwagon until the beginning of political Zionism.

Israel Zangwill
1864–1926

Born in London, Israel Zangwill wrote novels that concentrate primarily on Jewish themes. Perhaps his three most famous books are Children of the Ghetto *(1892),* Ghetto Tragedies *(1893), and* The King of Schnorrers *(1894).*

An early Zionist and member of the Order of the Ancient Maccabeans, a Zionist organization founded in 1891, he was an ardent admirer of Theodor Herzl and attended the First Congress (1897) in Basel, Switzerland, as well as subsequent conferences.

Zangwill was an advocate of a Jewish homeland wherever one could be secured and led a group of like-minded Zionists called the Territorialists. The Territorialists favored a Jewish homeland in Palestine, but felt that if Palestine could not be secured, any homeland was better than none at all.

Following the 1917 Balfour Declaration, in which Britain lent its support for a Jewish homeland in Palestine, the movement for a Jewish state outside of Palestine began to dwindle, and by 1925, the Territorialists had dissolved their group. Zangwill became a supporter of a Jewish homeland in Palestine and favored relocating local Arabs to neighboring Arab countries.

Zangwill died in 1926 in the city of Preston.

Daniel Deronda

An influential work of the nineteenth century, this novel about Jewish national aspirations was an early advocate of Zionism as well as a Jewish homeland in Palestine. Oddly enough it was written by George Eliot, the nom de plume of Marian Evans, an English Protestant, and author of many classics, including Silas Marner *and* The Mill on the Floss.

Raised in an evangelical Christian home, Evans was schooled in the Bible and its commentaries from an early age. An ardent philo-Semite who disdained the anti-Semitism of the day, she began to study Hebrew with Emmanuel Deutsch, a Talmudic scholar who worked at the British Museum. She and Deutsch, a passionate Zionist, became close friends and Deutsch became her mentor.

After Deutsch's death from cancer in 1870, Evans became even more enthralled with Judaism and spent years reading and visiting synagogues in preparation to write a Jewish novel. Daniel Deronda *was published in 1876 and its main character, Mordecai, was based on Emmanuel Deutsch.*

Daniel Deronda *awakened even assimilated Jews to the idea that they too could have a place to call home, just like the English among whom they lived.*

In 1899, the English Zionist Federation was formed and Sir Francis Montefiore was named as its leader. But many English Jewish leaders were less than taken with the idea and did not lend their support. Among them was Hermann Adler, England's Chief Rabbi. By the middle of World War I, that all changed and the leadership of British Jewry was actively pro-Zionist once they became convinced of the need for a Jewish homeland. Pro- and anti-Zionist forces within the community's leadership clashed just prior to the 1917 Balfour Declaration; the Zionist faction won and support for a Jewish national home in Palestine became policy.

The British had a political interest in placating both Jews and Arabs. Their interest in the former lay in a Palestinian Jewish community made up of Jews from postrevolutionary Russia and Poland with sentimental ties to Britain and its philanthropic Jewish leadership. This, they believed, would safeguard British Middle Eastern commerce, the Suez Canal, and their route to India. In 1917, at the time of the Balfour Declaration, the political situation in Russia was deteriorating rapidly and Great Britain and the other allies needed Russia to stay in the war in order to defeat the Germans. The British hoped that their support for Jewish national aspirations would encourage Jews in Russia to do what they could to keep Russia fighting. In addition, the British wanted to jump-start support for the war in a largely apathetic American Jewish community.

As for the Arabs, the international powers sought to curb pan-Islamism while retaining the cooperation of Arab leaders to facilitate Middle Eastern commerce. So the Balfour Declaration, while it viewed "with favour the establishment in Palestine of a national home for the Jewish people," stopped short of granting outright statehood in fear of alienating Britain's other equally important ally. It specifically stated that, though Britain supported Jewish aspirations, nothing could be done to abrogate the rights and privileges of other indigenous groups.

The Zionist organizations were nonetheless enthusiastic. But the Arabs, with whom Jewish settlers had lived in peace and cooperation since the late-nineteenth century, and who were undergoing their own rise of nationalism, became a little anxious.

In April 1920, Great Britain and France convened a meeting of the Supreme Council of the League of Nations in San Remo, Italy, to determine the future of the defeated Ottoman Empire. A continuation of a February 1920 conference in London, it gave control of Palestine (today's Israel and Jordan) and Mesopotamia (today's Iraq) to Great Britain, and what would later become Syria and Lebanon to France. And it endorsed the 1917 Balfour Declaration. By July 1922, the Balfour Declaration had become part of the British Mandate over Palestine.

During the 1920s, English Jewry became increasingly more English and more middle class. There was a mass movement away from places such as central London and its crowded East End to residential suburbs such as London's Golders Green with its houses and gardens. The children of immigrant Jews moved in even greater numbers into professions that had once been the realm of the upper-middle classes—medicine, law, accountancy, and university academics.

The Rise of Nazism and World War II

*D*URING THE 1930s, Fascism was becoming a strong political force in Europe. As a result, large numbers of refugees from Germany, Austria, Poland, Czechoslovakia, and Italy left their homes and found themselves in England—some 90,000 people in all.

England had its own homegrown Fascism—the black shirts—led by Sir Oswald Mosley. Up until the passage of the 1936 Public Order Act, Mosley and his band attacked Jews and Jewish property and led marches in Jewish neighborhoods. The result was a greater solidarity among England's Jews. This was coupled with the need to arrange aid for refugees and to raise money to continue settlements in Palestine.

World War II began on September 1, 1939, when Germany

invaded Poland. England's role as one of Germany's primary targets had a profound effect on England's Jews not only as Jews, but also as Englishmen. While men served in the armed forces, children were evacuated from London to safer places in the north of England away from major cities and industrial areas, and women worked in defense-related industries. Jewish life did not cease in London, but it was a fraction of what it had been, as communities sprang up in the countryside and in towns that previously had few or no Jews.

The East End of London, for centuries the hub of England's Jewish community, was devastated in the German Blitzkrieg. The incessant bombing, which began in the fall 1940, destroyed many Jewish buildings and institutions. Among the synagogues destroyed was the Great Synagogue in Duke's Place, and the Bevis Marks Synagogue, though not destroyed, was damaged. As a result of the Blitzkreig, precious little remains of the original Jewish neighborhoods, and by that time so many Jewish residents had moved out, that many buildings were never rebuilt (see chapter 2).

At the end of the war, some 40,000 to 50,000 mostly Jewish refugees from other parts of Europe were left in England. Their presence had a significant effect on English Jewry, as those middle-class refugees brought with them not only businesses—clothing, fur trade, pharmaceuticals, and engineering—but also an artistic community and a new intelligentsia. London replaced Leipzig, Germany, as Europe's center of fur trading, and groups of intellectuals and artists bolstered England's cultural life. Rabbis and scholars of Reform Judaism in Germany augmented England's Progressive Judaism movement, and, at the other end of the scale, England's Orthodox Jews were joined by members of Frankfurt's Orthodox community, which created a shift to the right within that segment of the population. Jewish day schools were strengthened and the immigrants were involved in virtually every academic field on the university level.

One result was the establishment of the Department of Hebrew and Jewish Studies at University College, London.

The end of World War II brought a grim recognition to the Jews of England. Despite having endured terrible destruction from German bombs at home and the loss of loved ones on the battlefield, England's Jews did not suffer under German occupation as did Jews in most of Europe—and they were not subject to imprisonment and murder in the concentration camps of the Third Reich.

But the war years and those immediately following placed a strain on the relationship between English Jews and their government. British foreign policy called for only the gradual institution of Jewish self-rule in Palestine and vacillated between appeasing the local Arab population and supporting the creation of a Jewish state. As a result, it was at direct odds with the interests and needs of English Jewry and, as it turned out, with the needs of the Jews of continental Europe.

For nearly two decades, the British rulers of Palestine, under their United Nations mandate, had been trying to accommodate both Jewish and Arab interests in the region. Proposals for cooperation came and went, but each one was rejected because it failed to satisfy either community. Through Arab anti-Jewish riots in the 1920s, commission reports, and seemingly endless negotiations with all parties, a workable solution remained elusive.

In 1929, Arab riots against the Jews of Palestine led Britain to establish two successive commissions under Sir Walter Shaw and Sir John Hope Simpson. Both found that Arab dissatisfaction was due to a growing fear that they would lose their land. Both commissions determined that the Arabs would be reassured by the imposition of restrictions on Jewish immigration and land acquisition. The result was a document known as the Passfield White Paper. The negative reaction on the part of

Palestinian Jews and Zionist leaders around the world was so strong that London was forced to rescind the decree.

Despite these difficulties, many in the British government truly believed that cooperation between the two groups was not only possible but also feasible, despite the increasingly adamant stand of both groups.

Throughout the 1920s and 1930s, riots and often violent protests against Jews became a hallmark of Palestine politics. The British were desperate for a solution, particularly as the growing Nazi persecution of German Jews was increasing the flow of Jewish refugees into Palestine.

The Arab High Committee, formed in 1936 to defend Palestine Arabs against what they perceived to be Jewish incursion, made good use of local Arab ignorance of German politics—politics of which Jews were acutely aware and fearful. The Arab ignorance of the German situation meant that the Arabs saw this only as a steady stream of Jewish settlers. But local Jews knew the number of immigrants was limited. The formation of the committee and the attacks against Jews it engendered was the immediate impetus for the establishment of the Royal Commission of Inquiry to Palestine and the appointment of Lord Robert Peel to study the situation. The Arab leadership refused to cooperate on any level.

The commission's 1937 report concluded that there was no hope of cooperation between Arabs and Jews in Palestine and that the idea of an inclusive national entity was not feasible. The report further recommended the partition of Palestine into separate Jewish and Arab states with the caveat that creating a state with a Jewish majority would involve such significant relocation of local Arabs as to render the partition solution extremely problematic.

By 1939, with Hitler making credible threats in Europe, and the Palestine Arabs unwilling to make any kind of accommodation regarding Jewish settlement there, Great Britain decided to settle the matter of Palestine—or so she thought.

In May 1939, a policy known as the White Paper was announced by the British government stating that Palestine would not be partitioned into separate Jewish and Arab states (as negotiators were trying to work out), but rather a dual national Palestinian State would come into being within ten years. During that ten-year period, Jews and Arabs would be asked to share an administrative role with the British. The White Paper stated further that Jewish immigration to Palestine would be limited to a total of 75,000 people for the next five years (the Jewish population of Palestine had risen from just under 84,000 in 1922 to 445,000 in 1939—some 30 percent of the total population). After that, Jewish immigration would be at the sufferance of the Arabs. In addition, Jewish land purchase in Palestine would be limited in some areas and forbidden in others. Jews and Arabs alike opposed this solution. England saw it as a way to keep a strategic and volatile piece of real estate from blowing up for the duration of a war that was imminent. But for Europe's millions of Jews, who would soon find themselves trapped in Nazi-dominated Europe with nowhere to go, England's timing could not have been worse. In the end, they were caught up in a nightmare from which millions would never awaken.

The Kindertransport

When it became obvious that Germany's Jews were trapped and there was no country willing to take them in, the British Jewish Refugee Committee made an appeal to some members of the British Parliament to allow children between the ages of five and seventeen into the country. After considerable debate, England agreed to admit an unspecified number of these children provided that a £50 bond would be posted for each child.

The first group left Germany just after Kristallnacht in

1938 and the last on September 3, 1939, just two days after the outbreak of the war. In all, some 10,000 children were able to leave Germany and thus survive the horrors that were to come.

The children were sent to a variety of places—foster families, orphanages—throughout England, Scotland, Wales, and Northern Ireland. Most were well treated, but most never saw their parents again.

The older ones joined the armed forces as soon as they were old enough.

Of the 10,000 nearly 25 percent eventually found their way to the United States and Canada.

Into the Arms of Strangers, a documentary about the Kindertransport, won the Academy Award for Best Documentary of 2000.

As it had during World War I, the issue of Palestine polarized the English Jewish community. Some felt that the community should stress the idea of a separate Jewish homeland while others felt that English Jewry's primary obligation was its allegiance to Great Britain. Though the two ideas were not mutually exclusive, the issue, coupled with rising concern over the welfare of Jews in the rest of Europe, made for tension within the Jewish community. This was exacerbated by the friction between the British authorities who oversaw Palestine, and the Yishuv, the Jewish government in Palestine. As a result, anti-Semitism began to emerge once again.

The Postwar Period

*T*HE THREE HUNDREDTH anniversary of Jewish resettlement in England was observed at London's Bevis Marks Synagogue in 1956 and celebrated at the Guildhall with such guests as the Duke of Edinburgh, the husband of Queen Elizabeth II. But this joint celebration in which all the branches of English Jewry participated masked some significant rifts in the community. Just eight years earlier, in 1948, when Sir Israel Brodie became the first Chief Rabbi to have been born and educated in England, he observed that English Jewry was polarized between the two extremes of observance—orthodoxy and liberalism. The middle seemed to be collapsing. On the Orthodox side, the numbers had increased with immigrants from Central and Eastern Europe before the Second World War. The liberal wing (Reform and Liberal) also gained membership from that same group of immigrants, but many also came from those who had moved away from Orthodox observance. And the character of English Jewry was continuing to change—from a largely urban, observant group centered in London's East End to a more affluent, suburban, and less observant community. This movement away from traditional observance had an effect on the level of participation in traditional synagogue organizations in that many retained their membership to maintain their burial rights but attended services closer to where they actually lived. Granted, the Orthodox, within their organizational framework of the United Synagogue, were abandoning some of their own relatively liberal tendencies and adopting a sort of neo-orthodoxy. But the bottom line was this: while the Orthodox were becoming more observant, the vast majority of Jews were becoming less so and retreating from Jewish identification of any kind.

The high degree of assimilation and Anglicization of British

Jewry notwithstanding, England was by no means free of anti-Jewish feeling or actions. Anti-Jewish groups desecrated and burnt synagogues in the late-1950s and mid-1960s, and discrimination existed in business and within the hallowed corridors of some of Britain's elite public (that is, private) schools, where Jews were subject to strict quotas. And, of course, there was the usual exclusion of Jews from private clubs. In reaction to such practices, the Council of Christians and Jews stepped up their efforts to promote better relations between Jews and non-Jews.

Had it not been for Israel and the social and community activity that surrounded things such as fund-raising, even more English Jews would have moved away from their religious affiliations. Indeed, as in other countries, Israel-centric activity has in some ways become a substitute for the religious-oriented activity of previous generations. This Israel-focused community life came to the fore with the Six-Day War of 1967, when the Jewish world as a whole, and English Jewry in particular, suddenly awakened to the mortal danger to Israel from its neighbors. Israel's victory was such an emotional event, even for Jews who had been previously unaffiliated and nonobservant, that it revitalized Jewish identity and the community.

At the time of the Six-Day War, there were some 400,000 Jews in Britain, with the majority of those living in and around London and other sizable pockets in the large cities. Though it never had the world's largest Jewish population, Britain did go from fourth to sixth place during the 1960s. As in other liberal societies, intermarriage and a declining birthrate continue to be major factors in the decline of the number of Jews in Great Britain.

Anti-Semitism had an upswing in the late-1970s with the rise of the extreme right-wing National Front. Founded in 1967, by members of the Racial Preservation Society, the British National Party, and the League of Empire Loyalists, they promoted a program of nationalism and white supremacy. In 1976, they garnered some 75,000 votes in local district council elections. Nationally, however, they did not do as well. In 1979, 301 of their candidates received just 191,000 votes and none was actually elected to a local council seat. But the unease was palpable, particularly as the National Front in France was gaining support—a campaign of hate that was punctuated by a synagogue bombing in Paris in 1980. As anti-Jewish sentiment tends to get worse during difficult economic times, the recession of the late 1970s and early 1980s only exacerbated the situation.

But anti-Semitism was not only a product of the extreme right; it was also an outgrowth of anti-Israel propaganda fomented by Britain's large Arab population. The November 1975 UN General Assembly resolution equating Zionism with racism was a springboard for an already vocal anti-Israel and anti-Jewish cadre of left-wingers, Palestinians, Arabs in general, and garden-variety anti-Semites to promulgate blatant anti-Semitic acts, particularly on university campuses, where recognition of Jewish student societies was taken away.

Today, there are approximately 300,000 Jews in the United Kingdom, with nearly two-thirds living in and around London. It is, by and large, a middle-and upper-middle-class community with hundreds of religious, charitable, and community organizations. Indeed, to take a quick look at the number and scope of Britain's Jewish organizations, one would think that the community is much larger than it actually is.

Jews today can be found in every occupation and in every social stratum, and though there has yet to be a Jewish occupant of 10 Downing Street, Jews are well represented in the political life of the country as members of Parliament, mayors, and cabinet ministers, and many have been made lords and knights.

Even so, the beginning of the twenty-first Christian century is a difficult time for the Jewish people in England, and elsewhere. Although there is unprecedented acceptance and participation in society at large—particularly in Western countries—the threat of complete assimilation is ever present even as the most Orthodox Jews gain strength and numbers.

British Jewry is undergoing the same sorts of problems and changes as the Jewish communities of other Western liberal societies—a high degree of assimilation, a high rate of intermarriage, and a movement away from the traditional Jewish life of their forebears. And, as in other countries, there is an increased polarization between those who try to assimilate completely and intermarry, and those who are moving back, little by little, to the faith of their fathers, even with the modern overtones of Reform and Liberal Judaism.

How British Jewry Is Organized— The Synagogue Movements

THE UNITED SYNAGOGUE

If anything represents the British Jewish establishment—not only to the British, but to the rest of the world—it is the United Synagogue. As its leader holds the title of Chief Rabbi of the United Hebrew Congregations of the British Commonwealth, how could anyone think anything else? But though the United Synagogue is one of the oldest synagogue groups in England and has the most affiliated synagogues, it is by no means the only representative of British Jewry.

United Synagogue is a group, albeit a large one, of Orthodox Ashkenazi shuls in London that began life in the nineteenth century as an association comprised of the Great Synagogue, the Hambro Synagogue, and the New Synagogue (see chapter 2). An

1870 act of Parliament gave it official status and today it is the largest in Britain.

During the period of immigration to England from Eastern Europe, the United Synagogue was in large part responsible for setting up programs and organizations designed to assist the new immigrants with learning English and education in general. Such generosity was tempered by the establishment's desire to change the roughhewn and extremely Orthodox ways of those they regarded as ignorant Yiddish-speaking peasants whom they generally viewed with disdain.

Once the new immigrants got their bearings, along with the education doled out by the United Synagogue, they began to resent the imposition of very English attitudes on a culture and way of life (the shtetl—small Eastern and Central European Jewish town) they thought worth preserving—even in this new country. The Yiddish-speaking immigrants attempted to re-create their way of life, and the unique form of Judaism it fostered, by forming small congregations, or chevrot. These stood in stark contrast to the large congregations of the United Synagogue, which the establishment didn't like one bit (see Federation of Synagogues, below).

Today the United Synagogue is the dominant English Jewish religious organization with some seventy synagogues totaling more than 100,000 members.

THE FEDERATION OF SYNAGOGUES

With the huge immigration of Jews to London's East End and the subsequent growth of the chevrot, the United Synagogue was apprehensive that so many small synagogues would lead to chaos. Then in stepped Samuel Montagu to ameliorate the situation. Montagu was a highly respected member of the United

Synagogue establishment who understood the animosity felt by the chevrot for their high-class brethren. Devising a set of minimum standards for size and hygiene, he organized the Federation of Minor Synagogues in 1887 and began combining synagogues that were too small into somewhat larger chevrot that still gave the members a sense of the shtetl life they left behind. In addition, he was instrumental in securing funding for the construction of new East End synagogues under Federation auspices.

Both organizations worked side by side for years until the early twentieth century when the debate within the Jewish community over Zionism created divisions once again. Where the Federation Jews were ardently Zionist, many of the old-line English Jewish leaders were not. Among the latter was the president of the Federation, Lord Swaythling, Samuel Montagu's son. In May 1917, a letter from the Board of Deputies and the Anglo-Jewish Association stating that British Jewry was not sympathetic to Zionism and the aims of the Balfour Declaration was published in the *London Times*. Needless to say, the members and board of the Federation were not pleased, and made no secret of their displeasure to the leadership. As a result, Lord Swaythling resigned in 1925.

As Zionism became more popular with the advent of World War II, Nazi crimes, and the establishment of the State of Israel, such arguments became irrelevant.

Though the Federation exists today with about a dozen synagogues in London, it is no longer the extremely Orthodox group it once was. The children, grandchildren, and great grandchildren of the original members have become assimilated, even if they do remain Orthodox. Those who still belong to Federation synagogues do so for a variety of reasons, including sentimentality or preference for a smaller shul.

THE UNION OF ORTHODOX HEBREW CONGREGATIONS

The extremely Orthodox, along with the various Hasidic sects, belong to the Union of Orthodox Hebrew Congregations.

Established in the 1880s by Jews who found the United Synagogue too liberal even in its orthodoxy, the UOHC synagogues were located in London's Stamford Hill district. In contrast to the highly centralized United Synagogue, however, today the Union is really a loose aggregate of highly independent shuls run by individual rabbis. Many of the early Union rabbis were followers of Rabbi Dr. Victor Schonefeld, himself a follower of Rabbi Samson Raphael Hirsch. Hirsch (1808–1888), a rabbi in Frankfurt, Germany, created the Frankfurt brand of Neo-Orthodox Judaism when he separated himself and his adherents from the German Reform movement. He advocated teaching traditional Jewish studies along with secular education. Today it is known as modern Orthodoxy.

THE REFORM SYNAGOGUES OF GREAT BRITAIN

In 1840, when eighteen highly respected members of the Bevis Marks Synagogue (see chapter 2) became dissatisfied with what they perceived as its rigidity, they reformed it—not much at the outset, but just enough to cause a stir. That stir is what became Reform Synagogues of Great Britain. For example, the reformers felt that not traveling on Shabbat was one thing, but having to schlep on foot from their new homes in more central parts of London to Bevis Marks was quite another. In addition, given their increasing level of Anglicization, they no longer found the long drawn-out, Hebrew-only services satisfying. They wanted another synagogue that more closely met their changing needs. Needless to say, the rabbinate at Bevis Marks took umbrage with their views, and rather than let the rebellious congregants set up a branch closer to their homes, they banned the rebels from any religious contact with other Jews— a prohibition known as a Cherem. In addition, they prohibited the establishment of a new synagogue within six miles of Bevis Marks.

British Reform is more akin to American Conservative than it is to American Reform—the service tends to be traditional, with a significant amount of Hebrew, but men and women sit together and women participate fully in the service. Indeed, many members of Reform wear yarmulkes, put on teffilin, and keep kosher, just like their Orthodox brethren.

THE UNION OF LIBERAL AND PROGRESSIVE SYNAGOGUES

Begun in 1902 by Claude Montefiore and the Honorable Lily Montagu (daughter of Samuel Montagu), the Union put an entirely new wrinkle on the face of British Jewry, and, initially, was not very welcome. Here, not only are men and women seated together, but men wear neither head covering nor tallit (traditional fringed prayer shawls). The service is in English and bears no resemblance to the traditional service either in content or in structure. Kashrut, a key component of traditional Judaism—even for British Reform Jews—is seen as archaic.

Until the rise of Nazism, this form of Judaism was anti-Zionist, but that changed after 1945. These days the Liberal and Progressive movement focuses on Judaism as a religion that embraces universal ethical concepts and does not stress a lot of ritual.

Where the traditional and Orthodox laws pertaining to conversion to Judaism are very strict, British Reform Jews tend to be more open, and the Liberals, who are even more open, accept the non-Jewish spouse in a mixed marriage into the congregation.

CHAPTER TWO

London

*E*NGLAND'S CAPITAL CITY has enough in it to keep you busy for years. London is one of the greatest cities in the world, and one of my personal favorites. I want to encourage you to get around on foot whenever possible—it's the best way to get to know London, and I have no doubt that you will come to love it as much as I do.

London has always had the largest of England's Jewish communities, and for centuries, the history of the Jews of London is in fact the history of the Jews of England. But London's, and indeed England's, Jewish community is hundreds of years younger than many in Europe, as Jewish settlement here began with the Norman Conquest of 1066.

In those early times, a few Jews probably had come over

from Normandy in France. There is some mention of a group of Jews in London in the latter part of the eleventh century, and records indicate that there was a Jewish quarter in the twelfth century—their cemetery was the sole Jewish burial ground in all of England. That group was collectively accused of murder in 1130 and fined an enormous sum.

Despite such difficulties, the community grew and prospered during the twelfth century under King Henry II (1154–89), as London became the destination for other Jews from continental Europe. But on September 3, 1189, a dreadful anti-Jewish riot broke out during the coronation of King Richard I. The riot began at the palace of Westminster and before long the Jewish quarter (in what is now the City) had been put to the torch. Thirty Jews died—a large number for such a small and closely knit community. As it would repeatedly through the years, the community held together in the face of adversity.

Richard I (1157–1199), of the House of Plantagenet, was the third son of King Henry II and Eleanor of Aquitaine and is known in history as Richard Lion Heart. During the Third Crusade, beginning in 1189, he (along with Philip II of France) captured Cyprus and parts of Palestine from the Muslim military leader Saladin. On his return to England from the Holy Land, Richard was captured by Austria's King Leopold in 1192 and held for ransom. In order to pay, King John, Richard's brother, who was keeping the throne warm in Richard's absence, raised the money by special taxes. A significant portion of the ransom was raised from within the Jewish community—the Jews of London contributed some 25 percent of the entire Jewish levy.

The loss of recorded transactions with Jewish financiers during anti-Jewish riots was a problem for the Crown. As the Crown did so much business with Jews, something had to be done to protect those records. Under Richard's reign, an administrative mechanism for creating duplicate and thus more secure records was set up—called the Ordinance of the Jewry—and its central office in London oversaw the regional offices.

The thirteenth century was not a good one for the Jews of London, and the years leading up to the expulsion in 1290 were brutal.

During the reign of King John (1199–1216), there were more anti-Jewish outbreaks in London. This was due in part to the so-called Barons' War, when resentment of Jewish financial connections to the Crown boiled over and resulted in a number of attacks including one on the London Jewish community in 1215. It should be noted that the barons' opposition was not just to Jewish involvement with the royal coffers, but to what was perceived as royal financial malfeasance.

Shaky financial (and other) dealings by the government continued into the reign of Henry III (1216–72), as did anti-Jewish acts. Huge taxes and fines were imposed on the Jews of London and on the Jews in the rest of the country, and edicts restricting activity were implemented. In 1244, when a dead child was found in London with slash marks all over its body, it was alleged that those marks were Hebrew letters. A ritual murder charge resulted in an enormous monetary penalty on the Jewish community.

King Henry confiscated the main London synagogue in 1232 to prevent Jewish chanting from disturbing those in a nearby church. Not content with that, he established the Domus Conversorum—an office to promote Jewish conversion to Christianity and house the converts.

During the thirteenth century, as many as five hundred Jews lived in London, although sources differ on the exact number and some contemporary accounts place it as high as two thousand families. The Jewish quarter was located in the City in an area known as the "Jewry." Today, all that's left of the quarter is its name—Old Jewry Street, located right near the Aldgate tube stop, which you will visit later in the walking tour.

Simon de Montfort (1208–65) may be credited with the formation of what would become England's modern Parliament, but he was no friend of the Jews. But then neither was his father, who led the crusade against the Christian heretic Albigenses in France in which hundreds of Jews were slaughtered. De Montfort the elder and his followers took an oath "to forever removing the Jews from all administration and office, not ever to restore them, nor to accept other Jews for any office . . . nor use their council against Christians, nor . . . to permit them to employ Christians, men or women, in their homes as servants."[5]

De Montfort the younger took after his father and was personally responsible for numerous murders and anti-Jewish riots. As leader of the opposition to King Henry III, he destroyed much of London's Jewish quarter as well as the Jewish quarters of cities such as Winchester on the most trivial of pretexts—a dispute over a debt between a Jew and a non-Jew in 1263, or the rumor that Jews manufactured explosives for the king's troops.

A short period of calm for the Jewish community attended the end of the Baron's war and the accession of Edward I. But it was a calm before yet another storm.

Edward I's Statutum de Judaismo (1275) forbade Jews from earning a living as moneylenders. By that time, Jewish wealth had already been greatly diminished and the money-lending business had been taken over by bankers from elsewhere in Europe. Because Jews no longer provided a large source of revenue to the Crown, the Statutum gave Jews the right to engage in other forms of commerce—but only on a trial basis. However, though legally Jews could practice other forms of commerce, the prohibition of Jewish membership in the Guild Merchant meant that those other forms of commerce would remain closed. As a result, Jews were forced to engage secretly in money lending and some resorted to clipping coins (see page 8). Hundreds were imprisoned in the Tower of London for coin clipping and many were hanged for it, including some Jews who had committed no crime at all.

The year 1281 saw yet another ritual murder charge and a resulting order restricted Jewish residence in London to the Jewry. Two years later, all synagogues in London were ordered closed by the local Bishop.

Frustrated that the Statutum de Judaismo had failed to achieve its goal, and beset by difficult economic and political problems, Edward I expelled the Jews from England on July 18, 1290. The relatively small Jewish community of approximately four thousand moved to France, Germany, and Flanders. Jews would not live in England again until the seventeenth century.

Between the Expulsion, as this period was known, and the Resettlement, England was not completely devoid of Jews. Several dozen converts continued to live under the auspices of Henry III's Domus Conversorum, some Jews were permitted to enter England provided they converted to Christianity, and a few Jewish physicians resided in London during the fifteenth century. Conversos (see page 8) fleeing the Inquisition in Spain and Portugal found their way to London in the fifteenth century and continued to be Christian in public and Jewish in secret. By the time of Henry VIII's (1491–1547) death, there were thirty-seven such families living in London and attending services at the home of the community's leader, Alves Lopes. Two of the most prominent members of that community were Queen Elizabeth I's (1558–1603) physician, Roderigo Lopez, and royal financial adviser Hector Nunez. Lopez was beheaded under suspicion that he had tried to poison the queen.

By 1609, London's dalliance with Jews ended when the refugees from Spain and Portugal were accused of Judaizing (that is, practicing Judaism in private while outwardly practicing Christianity) and expelled.

The Resettlement

THIRTY-THREE YEARS AFTER that second and final expulsion, events in France, Spain, and Portugal would lay a foundation for the reestablishment of a Jewish community in England.

Abraham Israel Carvajal was born Antonio Fernandez in Portugal in 1590. The son of a Converso family, he became a merchant and eventually settled in Rouen, France. In 1633, when Rouen's Conversos were expelled for Judaizing, Carvajal went to London (using his non-Jewish name), where he was a large-scale shipper and trader in goods from the East and West Indies. He serviced the parliamentary faction during the English civil war and gained the confidence of Oliver Cromwell, for whom he gathered foreign intelligence.

By the time Manasseh ben Israel came to England in 1655 to petition Oliver Cromwell to readmit the Jews, there was a community of secret Jews there to greet him with Carvajal as its leader. That initial bid for readmission failed, but there was enough support to justify a smaller move—Jewish worship out in the open. Cromwell was successfully petitioned to protect this free worship in 1656. As a result, the erstwhile secret Jews rented a building to use as a synagogue (on London's Creechurch Lane) and soon after a plot of land for a cemetery was purchased.

Although Oliver Cromwell's death saw attempts once again to expel the Jews from England, King Charles II interceded on their behalf. The synagogue was enlarged in 1674, and in 1701 the present (and larger) synagogue on Bevis Marks was built.

During the seventeenth century the Sephardic Jews grew and prospered, taking in immigrants from Spain and Portugal, who continued to be persecuted by the Inquisition. In the latter part of the century, large numbers of Sephardim from Holland, descendents of early refugees from Spain and Portugal, began to arrive. For the most part, the men of the community were merchants and brokers, though there were a few physicians as well.

In 1697, the first Jewish brokers were admitted to the Royal Exchange, although their number was limited to twelve. In order to maintain their small foothold in this all-important commercial venue, the community had to pay a tribute to the Lord Mayor. Each year the leaders of the community would, with great ceremony, present his lordship with fifty guineas.

Around the same time as the Sephardic Jews were coming to England from Holland, a number of Ashkenazim (Jews from Eastern and Central Europe) were also making their way to London, and by 1690 they had their own congregation. Six years later, one of the wealthy elders of the community, Benjamin Levy, secured ground for a cemetery. The original Ashkenazi synagogue, which was located on Duke's Place in the City, was reconstructed in 1722 by Moses Hart. Hart was the brother of Aaron Hart (Rabbi Uri Phoebus ben Naphtali Hirsch), one of England's early rabbis. The synagogue was enlarged again in 1766 and in 1790. But in 1706, a disagreement led to the establishment of another community, which built the Hambro Synagogue in 1726. Yet another split resulted in the formation of the New Synagogue in 1761.

By the middle of the eighteenth century, the Ashkenazi Jews outnumbered their Sephardi counterparts and constituted the foundation of London Jewry. Of course not all the Ashkenazi immigrants were wealthy or even what would now be considered middle class—they were mainly peddlers and rag dealers, and they were accused of being responsible for more than their fair share of crime.

With a degree of security never before known in England, the Jews of the nineteenth century started to expand. More synagogues were established outside the City and the East End and other community organizations were rethinking the way they were constituted. Full emancipation was still elusive, but it would be a fact by the end of the century.

A joint Ashkenazi and Sephardi board for the oversight of kosher food (shechita) was established in 1792; the Board of Deputies of British Jews, which exists to this day, was formed out of the Sephardi community's Committee of Deputados. The Deputados, an ad hoc group empowered to represent the Jewish community to the Crown, included some Ashkenazim in their numbers as early as 1760. In 1838, the Board of Deputies itself was expanded to include Jews outside of London. The Jews' Free School, established in 1817, grew out of the Ashkenazi Talmud Torah that dated back to 1732.

Despite obvious progress, full civil rights remained an unfulfilled dream. Jews were not permitted to engage in retail trade until 1831. But in 1835 the first Jew, David Salomons, was elected sheriff of London; in 1847, he became London's first Jewish alderman; and finally, in 1855, London's first Jewish Lord Mayor. There were still major impediments to equality, however. And nowhere could that be seen more clearly than in the case of Baron Lionel de Rothschild. Though the City of London had begun electing Rothschild as its representative to the House of Commons in 1830, he could not formally take his seat because the House of Lords continually blocked legislation that would change the parliamentary oath—an oath that required swearing on one's true faith as a Christian.

The immigration of Russian Jews in the late-nineteenth century increased the London Jewish population threefold—from about 47,000 prior to 1881 to some 150,000. Of those, two-thirds lived in London's East End. The immigrants were poor—mainly tailors, shoemakers, and cabinetmakers—hardly at the social level the old-timers had achieved. And they were overwhelmingly Orthodox, which was something some of the established English Jews had begun to move away from. Still, the establishment Jews took their brethren under their wing and saw to it that they were provided for through charities. The newcomers themselves began to establish their own services and organizations—a Yiddish press, a trade union movement, and small synagogues.

As in other countries, there was a tendency of those who came before to exploit new immigrants—preying on their unfamiliarity with language and customs, and capitalizing on their fear of being sent back to an even less hospitable country. This was the case with the Russian Jewish immigrants to England. In 1889, 10,000 Jewish tailors went on strike for six weeks to protest their treatment at the hands of their primarily Jewish employers, and the resulting publicity ended much of the widespread abuses.

And also as in other countries, there was a tendency of those who came before to attribute society's ills to new immigrants. The Russian Jews were accused of driving down wages and driving up rents in the slummy East End. Though a Royal Commission on Alien Immigration found such charges to be without merit, that did not allay the fears of non-Jewish East End residents, who led nearly as precarious a life as the newcomers.

Jake the Ripper?

Everyone loves an unsolved mystery. And in the annals of unsolved mysteries, the Whitechapel murders, the infamous case of Jack the Ripper, are among those where countless theories abound and about which volumes have been written.

Jack the Ripper was the press's nickname for a serial killer in East London's Whitechapel district who murdered and mutilated five prostitutes between August 31 and November 9, 1888. Some theories say it was more than five.

One of the theories about Jack's identity is that he was a shochet (ritual slaughterer of animals used for kosher meat). As a shochet in a neighborhood with a very large Jewish population, as Whitechapel was at the time, his bloodstained apron would have gone unnoticed. But it was also a neighborhood of filth, poverty, prostitutes, thieves, and other criminal types. One of the identifying characteristics of the Ripper murders was the perpetrator's obvious knowledge of anatomy—something a shochet would have had to have. The victims had their throats cut and in many cases the mutilation involved the sexual organs and the removal of other organs along with hunks of flesh.

An actual Jewish suspect was Aaron Kosminski, a Polish immigrant who lived in Whitechapel and was known to hate women, but who, according to records, had no knowledge of anatomy. The only actual evidence against him was a flimsy identification by an alleged witness to one of the murders. Kosminski was sent to Colney Hatch Asylum in February of 1891 for three years, as—even if he was innocent of the murders in question—he was deemed to be insane. He was released and later sent to the Leavesden Asylum, a home for the insane where he died in 1919.

There was some eagerness on the part of the police and the public to pin the murders on a Jew and some chronicles of the Ripper crimes point, not unjustly, to an anti-Jewish bias on the part of Scotland Yard. At the time there was a great deal of backlash against the Russian and Polish Jewish immigrants who seemed to be flooding England and settling overwhelmingly in London's East End. There was widespread fear that not only did the Jews generate crime, but that those new, foreign Jews were dirty and represented the most unsavory characteristics of human behavior.

Most of the theories as to the identity of Jack the Ripper involve non-Jews and we will probably never know the entire story.

In order to curb immigration, Parliament passed the Aliens Act of 1905. However, the act still allowed political refugees to gain admission and Jews fleeing Russian pogroms continued to enter England until the eve of World War I in 1914. By that time, the earlier generation of immigrants had become more well-to-do and had begun moving to the suburbs—especially to Golders Green in northwest London and Stamford Hill in northeast London. Today, those areas are large and thriving Jewish communities.

The movement of Jews to the suburbs continued in the interwar period. The rise of Nazism brought new immigrants of a different economic level than those of the previous generation. The refugees from Germany were for the most part middle class or professional, and they were instrumental in revitalizing not only economic but cultural life as well.

England did not escape Fascism, though it never really took hold there. In the 1930s, Sir Oswald Mosley and his British Union of Fascists—known as Blackshirts—were responsible for several anti-Jewish attacks. In 1936, they marched through London's East End. Thousands turned out in protest—Jew and non-Jew alike. In 1936, the Public Order Act banned the wearing of political uniforms, which put an end to some of the Blackshirts' activities.

The Blitzkrieg played a major role in destroying the City and the East End of London. Large areas were nearly obliterated by German bombs, including what was the center of the Jewish population. Many Jews escaped to the safety of less central parts of town and by the end of World War II, the more prosperous Jewish community had no need to rebuild in the East End.

The trend out of the East End grew in the 1950s and 1960s as the Jewish population there continued to decline. At the beginning of the twentieth century, the East End was home to about 150,000 Jews; by 1929, the number was 85,000; and by 1950, only some 30,000 remained. Today estimates vary wildly, but some figures put the population at around 3,000 mostly elderly Jews. The vast majority of London's Jews live in the northern suburbs. In the 1990s, the borough of Barnet in the northwest emerged as one of the largest Jewish areas. Redbridge, east of London, is the second-largest community.

But geographical expansion has not meant a numerical expansion. In fact, the Jewish population of London, and of England in general, has declined since the mid-1970s due to a decreased birthrate, high intermarriage, and a general movement away from Judaism. A population of 221,000 in 1975 dropped to 210,000 by 1988, and to 185,000 by 1996. The Jewish population of England as a whole hit its high of 420,000 in 1950 and now stands at about 280,000.

Despite declining numbers, London continues to be the center of Jewish life in England—though it doesn't have the hegemony it once had—and Manchester is giving it a run for its money.

London Sights

THE EAST END

Once upon a time, the East End of London was to British Jews what the Lower East Side of Manhattan was to American Jews. Dozens of synagogues and organizations, along with tens of thousands of Jews, could be found in a relatively small area of what is known as the East End. Within that area are Whitechapel, Spitalfields, Stepney, and Shoreditch—all of which at one time were home to thriving Jewish communities.

Today, a fraction of this population remains, the result of Jewish upward mobility. Jews in England have prospered and

Commercial Road Talmud Torah on Christian Street
in London's East End (closed 1980). *Roger Cowen*

moved to more fashionable areas of town and to the suburbs.
Unfortunately, not many Jewish buildings remain. Vast sections
of these neighborhoods were completely destroyed by German
bombs during World War II and urban renewal following the
war did much to clean up what was left of a pretty unsavory district. But today, as in most large cities, parts of East End neighborhoods are undergoing gentrification and some Jews are
moving back. Some old buildings are being turned into pricey
and elegant houses—a far cry from the squalid flats their forebears called home.

Soup kitchen for the Jewish poor, Brune Street in
London's East End (closed 1993). *Roger Cowen*

Walking Tour

On this walking tour you'll see most of what is left of the
Jewish East End. Wear your walking shoes, and bring along your
copy of *London A–Z*—the streets can be confusing, so it's a
MUST. And as this is London, it's best to bring the umbrella.

Few synagogues and only a relative handful of Jews remain
today in London's East End. Parts of this ancient area (the original city of London) have been home to Jews for centuries—both
before and after the official expulsion of Jews in 1290. Early in
the twentieth century, some 150,000 Jews lived here in places
such as Whitechapel, Stepney, and Spitalfields.

Not far from where the City of London ends and the East

End begins, England's first Jews built their synagogue in Creechurch Lane and later, the renowned Sephardic shul, Shar HaShamayim, in a street called Bevis Marks.

Only scant remnants of that community can be seen today. In most cases, only the names of some streets remind us that this area of old London was Jewish—Jewry street. Old Jewry further to the west, and the Church of St. Lawrence Jewry, so named because it was a church in a Jewish quarter.

The Jews who remain here, who still call the East End home, now live among a Muslim population—the result of a latter-day immigration of Bengalis, Pakistanis, and assorted Arabs. Some synagogues have been converted into mosques; many of those, such as the one at the corner of Brick Lane and Fournier Street, preach a fundamentalist Islam that has no use for outsiders.

Starting point: Aldgate Tube Station (Circle Line; Metropolitan Line)—not to be confused with the Aldgate East Station.

When you come out of the tube station, you will be on Aldgate High Street. This turns into Whitechapel High Street, the Whitechapel Road, and then Mile End Road.

Our first stop is the famous synagogue on Bevis Marks, then will proceed to most of what is left of the Jewish East End.

With your back to the tube station, turn right and walk to the Parish Church of St. Botolph's Aldgate at the end of the block. Cross over to the traffic island, and just across Aldgate High Street, you'll see a street sign that says Jewry Street. This area of London, known as the City, London's financial center, was where Jews settled both before the Expulsion and after the Resettlement. Most of the buildings you see around you are fairly new, as this section of town was almost totally destroyed by German bombs during World War II and precious little of old London town remains. Before the Expulsion, in the twelfth and thirteenth centuries, there was a number of synagogues a short distance to the west—on Old Jewry Street, just off Cheapside and on Leadenhall Street.

Soup kitchen for the Jewish poor, Brune Street in
London's East End (closed 1993). *Roger Cowen*

On the traffic island stay to your right, cross the street, and
make an immediate right turn onto Duke's Place, which is
unmarked at this point. It was in this street that the first Ashkenazi synagogue of London was founded in 1690. Over the
decades it underwent various changes such as enlarging and
reconstruction. Known as the **Great Synagogue**, or the Duke's
Place shul, it was not only a synagogue but also the community's
heart and center, and it was known throughout the world. It was
completely obliterated by German bombs during World War II,
as was old Duke's Place itself.

Not far to the west, on Fenchurch Street, was the **Hambro
Synagogue**. Founded by dissenting members of the Great Synagogue, it was built between 1721 and 1726 and stood on the

same site until 1892. After that the congregation moved to a new building on Union Street, just off Commercial Road in Whitechapel, an area we'll visit later. In the 1930s, the membership decided to return home, as it were, and merged with the Great Synagogue.

The **New Synagogue** was also nearby on St. Helen's Street, just off Bishopsgate. Now located in Stamford Hill, it has been moved several times over the decades, but it is now in danger of disappearing due to lack of use. Here is what the Survey of the Jewish Built Heritage has to say about it:

> An Edwardian replica of the historic Great St. Helen's Synagogue in the City of London, designed by John

Cheshire Street Synagogue in London's East End (closed 1988). *Roger Cowen*

Davies in 1838 and containing some original fixtures from that building. These include the concave Ark, inspired by that of the now lost Great Synagogue of James Spiller (1760). Sold by the United Synagogue in the late 1980s, the building stands virtually redundant. It was recorded by the Survey in 1996 and, listed Grade II, was added to the English Heritage Listed Buildings at Risk register.[6]

As you walk along Duke's Place, you will pass Creechurch Lane. This was the site of the first synagogue after the Resettlement. It opened in 1656—services were held in the upper floors of a house at number 5. The building remained until it was torn down in 1857. The Sephardic congregation that worshiped here soon grew too large for its quarters and the synagogue at Bevis Marks was built.

At Creechurch Lane, Duke's Place becomes Bevis Marks. The name Bevis is believed to be a corruption of the town Bury St. Edmonds, whose Abbot owned the land in this district. Marks indicates its boundary line.

A few feet ahead, on your left, is a small, iron-gated entryway in the middle of a strip of modern buildings—this is the entry to the synagogue.

Bevis Marks Synagogue (Shar HaShamayim, Gate of Heaven). Contact information: The Spanish and Portuguese Jews' Congregation, 2 Heneage Lane, London, EC3A 5DQ. Tel: 020-7626-1274; E-mail bevismarks@first-step.demon.co.uk.

Visiting hours are Monday, Tuesday, Wednesday, Friday, and Sunday, 11:30 AM–1 PM. Services are held Monday and Thursday at 7:30 AM; Saturday at 8:30 AM, and Sunday at 9 AM. No tourists will be admitted during services. In addition to the actual synagogue, there is a small museum in the administration offices at 2 Heneage Lane. It's a good idea to make arrangements for a visit prior to your arrival.

Built on a plot of leased land known as the Plough Yard, Bevis Marks was completed in 1701. This is the second synagogue to have been built after the Jews were readmitted to England. Today it is the oldest synagogue in England that is still in use as such and contains some of the furnishings from the Creechurch Lane building, including some of the Puritan-style benches. They are still used and are amazingly strong.

As a result of ongoing maintenance, the building today looks very much like it did in the eighteenth century, apart from the addition of choir stalls at the back of the reader's platform in 1839. The synagogue's interior is Puritan neoclassical, the style of the period. Its layout is the same as the layout of the Creechurch Lane synagogue, and the structure was actually built by a Quaker, Joseph Avis. It looks very much like other religious houses of the same period. The Jewish community of Amsterdam donated many of the synagogue's fixtures. You won't see much in the way of Jewish decorations inside, apart from the Hebrew on the Aron Kodesh (the Ark)

A major restoration was begun in 1992, when it was discovered that the floor was rotting. But it is interesting to note that the rot came not with age, but as a result of carpeting put in for a wedding in 1990. Apparently, the carpet was installed without proper supervision or proper ventilation and was glued directly onto the three-hundred-year-old wooden floor. As a result of the disaster, a lot of the original wood was lost.

But sometimes shoddy workmanship has its advantages. Soon after the new floor was installed, the IRA bombed the nearby Baltic Exchange. The blast was so strong that it caused damage to the synagogue and could have caused its collapse if the new floor had not been in place. Windows were blown out, and some of the window jambs were forced from the walls. It was not the synagogue's first bomb damage. Back in 1915, during World War I, a bomb exploded in the courtyard during Kol Nidre services (the beginning of Yom Kippur). Fortunately, Bevis Marks escaped the bombs that leveled the nearby Great Synagogue during World War II.

Retrace your steps back along Bevis Marks to the corner of Creechurch Lane and Duke's Place. Cross the street to your left and walk up Creechurch Lane. Cross the street at Houndsditch, which is perpendicular to Creechurch Lane; at that point Creechurch Lane becomes Stoney Lane. Walk one block to the corner of White Kennett Street, turn right, and then make the first left onto Gravel Lane. The next street, perpendicular to Gravel Lane, is Middlesex Street, also known as Petticoat Lane. Turn left here.

Today's Petticoat Lane street market doesn't look all that different from the way it did in the days when it was primarily a street of Jewish merchants selling old clothing, housewares, food, and just plain junk. Today the Jews are gone, but the wares being sold haven't changed much. These days, mostly Muslims, who are now the majority in the area, run the stalls.

Continue north along Petticoat Lane to the corner of Frying Pan Alley and Sandy's Row, which veers off to your right. This district is known as Spitalfields—a corruption of Hospital Fields, for the London hospital nearby.

Walk up Sandy's Row. You'll see lots of old London here—colorful pubs, and narrow, winding streets.

On your right, just before the end of the street, is the **Sandy's Row Synagogue**. Tel: 020-7253-8311.

Services are held daily and on Shabbat and festivals. Call for exact times. The congregation, established in 1854 by a group of Jews from Holland, was meant to serve as a kind of workingman's synagogue in contradistinction to the Great Synagogue, whose members tended to be wealthier. The congregation's first homes were in various Spitalfields buildings, including Zetland Hall in Mansell Street. In 1867, the congregation took over the French Chapel on Artillery Lane, perpendicular to Sandy's Row. Three years later, they were able to raise enough funds to make repairs to the building and open a new entrance on Sandy's Row. This was no easy feat. This workingman's shul was not looked upon too kindly by the elders at the nearby Great Synagogue, who felt that there was no need for another synagogue in the area and who objected to seats being offered at low fees. But Sandy's Row, unwilling to let Jews with less means relinquish control over their community life to the richer congregation, prevailed. At the end of the nineteenth and beginning of the twentieth centuries, Sandy's Row was affiliated with the Great Synagogue for burial purposes. But in 1949, it once again became independent and remains so to this day.

At the top of Sandy's Row, turn right onto Artillery Lane, then left onto unmarked Steward Street—the first street after Fort Street (the first street on your left after you leave Sandy's Row). At the end of Steward Street, turn right onto Brushfield Street. The Spitalfields covered market is on your left. Inside, you'll find stalls selling food from all over the world (nothing kosher as of early 2001), souvenirs, and the usual flea-market type of clothing and bric-a-brac. You will also find a public toilet here.

Continue along Brushfield Street to Commercial Street (not to be confused with Commercial Road, which we will get to later) and make a left. Walk one block to Lamb Street, cross Commercial Street, and continue on into Hanbury Street. Walk one block and make a right turn onto Wilkes Street. As you walk, look around you. Notice the Arabic street signs along with the English ones. Make a left turn onto the first street you come to—Princelet Street—it's unmarked at this end.

As you walk along Princelet Street, look carefully at some of the doorposts on the right-hand side of the street. You can still see painted-over mezuzahs or their outlines in this once-heavily Jewish neighborhood—number 18 and number 20 in particular. Number 9 was the home, between 1916 and 1919, of Rav Avraham Yitzhak Kook (1865–1935), the rabbinic scholar who didn't have much use for England and became Chief Rabbi of Palestine in 1921. Rav Kook was the rabbi of the Spitalfields Great Synagogue that we'll see in a few minutes. Directly across the street was a Yiddish theater.

At number 19 is the **Princelet Street Synagogue**.

In use from 1862 until 1983, it is being restored and converted into a museum dedicated to all of London's East End immigrants, not only Jews. At press time the museum was far from completion and visiting hours are very irregular and usually granted by appointment only under special circumstances.

The building itself dates back to 1718 and once was a private house owned by a Huguenot (French Protestant) silk weaver. In 1862, a congregation from nearby Fashion Street took over the building, extended it over the back garden, and called it the United Friends' Synagogue. The congregation was made up mainly of Jews from the garment business and the simplicity of the synagogue's interior itself reflected their limited means.

Continue to the corner of Princelet Street and turn right onto Brick Lane. On the next corner, Fournier Street, is a large mosque. *Note:* Don't even think about going inside. This is a very orthodox Muslim congregation and they don't take kindly to outsiders.

This used to be the **Spitalfields Great Synagogue**.

Established in 1898 as the Machzikei Hadath Kehilla, it had been a Huguenot chapel that was built in 1743. This community was a breakaway group that was dissatisfied with the level of orthodoxy of the more established synagogues and Jewish authorities. Based on the Eastern European Beth Haknesset model—a place not only for prayer, but for meeting and for study—the synagogue was meant as an antidote for what some regarded as the liberalizing trend of England's Jewish community. When the Jewish community took over the building, they maintained the exterior, but remodeled the interior. Today, the exterior is still pretty much intact.

Continue along Brick Lane. This was once the commercial heart of the Jewish East End, and if you look carefully you can still see some vestiges of Jewish establishments. Number 92 is the establishment of N. Katz while number 78 bears the name Lederman. Messers Marx and Minser hold forth upstairs at the corner of Fashion Street and Brick Lane; number 17 still houses a Jewish monument company.

Brick Lane becomes Osborn Street and then ends at Whitechapel High Street. Cross Osborne Street to your left, then take the first crosswalk and cross over what is now Whitechapel Road and turn left on the other side. On your right, a short way along, is Adler Street, which is named for England's former chief rabbi.

Just south is Cable Street. It was here that an infamous confrontation between the British Union of Fascists and the local populace took place on October 4, 1936.

The borough of Stepney, in which Cable Street is located, was home to most of the East End's Jews at the time. Nearly 60,000 Jews lived in the borough. As social conditions worsened during the worldwide depression, Fascism was rising not only in continental Europe but in England too.

Oswald Mosely and his black-shirted British Union of Fascists were no different in philosophy than their continental counterparts: They blamed Jews for the world's ills. Stepney, with its huge Jewish population, was to be a showcase for a demonstration of Fascist power on October 4, 1936. But Mosely and his gang were not victorious that day as Jews, trade unionists, Communists, and members of organized labor, working in concert, beat back the Fascist demonstrators in a show of their own strength.

The Little Synagogue and the Great Big Mosque
Continue along Whitechapel Road to Fieldgate Street, which then veers off ahead to the left. On the corner of Whitechapel and Fieldgate is the Whitechapel Bell Foundry—this was where the Liberty Bell was cast in 1752. You are now in the borough of Stepney.

At number 41 is the **Fieldgate Street Great Synagogue** (Tel: 020-7247-2644).

Next door, and towering over the little shul, is the large East London mosque—a testament to the new character of the neighborhood. The friendliness of the people who hang out in front of the mosque, mostly Muslims from Asia, may depend on the current state of Middle East affairs. On a visit early in 2000, one caftaned gentleman suggested that I take the photos I was shooting to Israel to show the Israelis how well Jews and Muslims get along. But a visit in 2001 was far less agreeable—the synagogue had just been cleaned of anti-Semitic and anti-Israel graffiti.

The original synagogue was established in 1899; it was damaged by bombing during World War II and rebuilt in 1950. Today it has a membership of several hundred, which is comprised mostly of members of other East End synagogues that have since closed as well as those who have moved to the suburbs but maintain their burial rights here.

If you are of a mind to do so, you might want to come here for Shabbat services. Not only will you hear traditional Jewish chanting, but your own prayers will be punctuated by the call of the muezzin from the mosque—the Muslim morning prayers coincide with Shacharit. It's either funny or mildly surreal, depending on your perspective.

Fair warning! There's not much of this tour left, but it's a bit of a schlep to continue. If you want to stop, you can end the walk here, and retrace your steps back to Whitechapel Road, and get the Hammersmith and City Line or the District Line at the Aldgate East tube stop.

If you want to continue, walk along Fieldgate Street to New Road and turn right. Continue along New Road for a few blocks to Nelson Street, which will be on your left.

At number 30/40 is the **East London Central Synagogue** (Tel: 020-7790-9809).

> Founded in 1923, this shul still gets around thirty people on a Saturday morning and is filled to capacity on Rosh Hashanah and Yom Kippur. Most of the attendees don't live in the neighborhood—they come in from the suburbs. Above the iron gate is a stone that says Nelson Street Sephardish Synagogue. This doesn't mean the same thing as Sephardic. Sephardish refers to the form of prayers used by some Hassidic sects, but also some non-Hassidic Orthodox Jews. Like Sephardic, its origins are in Spain.

Retrace your steps back to New Road, turn left, continue to Commercial Road, and make another left turn.

At number 351/355 Commercial Road is the **Congregation of Jacob,** built in 1920. Inquiries can be made to the secretary, Mr. DaCosta (Tel: 0958-486792).

> Established in 1904 with a congregation of immigrants from Eastern Europe, this synagogue has a tired-looking exterior

that conceals a friendly shul made up of mostly elderly Jews. There is barely a minyan on Shabbat, but they get a bigger crowd for Rosh Hashanah and Yom Kippur.

The walk ends here. The nearest tube stop is Whitechapel. Make a left turn onto Cavell Street and then when you get to Whitechapel Road, make a left. Trains here are on the Hammersmith and City Line and the District Line. Or, if you're tired of walking, cross to the other side of Commercial Road where you'll find a bus stop a block or two to your left. From there the #15 bus going in the direction of Paddington will take you back to the Aldgate tube stop. *Do not* take the #15 bus that stops on the same side of the street as the synagogue.

East End Jewish Cemeteries

There are a number of very old cemeteries in the East End. None are in current use, but sometimes arrangements to visit them can be made by calling the numbers listed below. You may be able to combine a cemetery visit with your walking tour.

Beth Haim Velho. 253 Mile End Road, E1. Opened in 1657 and the oldest Jewish cemetery in the UK.

Beth Haim Nuevo. 329 Mile End Road, E1. Opened in 1725. The phone number for both is 020-8455-2569.

Alderney Road Cemetery. E1. Tel: 020-7790-1445. Opened in 1696 for the Great Synagogue.

Brady Street. E1. Tel: 020-8985-1527. Opened in 1761 for the New Synagogue and later used by the Great Synagogue.

Grave of David Mocatta, philanthropist and founder of the
West London Synagogue. *David Jacobs*

WEST, CENTRAL, AND NEAR CENTRAL LONDON

The West London Synagogue. 34 Upper Berkeley
Street, W1. Tel: 020-7723-4404. (British) Reform. Call
for service times. Tube: Marble Arch.

Built in 1870 by a congregation that was established in 1840,
this is one of the most beautiful synagogues in England. Its
founders were members of the Spanish and Portuguese
synagogue in Bevis Marks who found aspects of the strict
Orthodox ways of that congregation disagreeable and wanted
something that was more in harmony with their daily lives
while still true to Jewish tradition. These dissenters formed the
nucleus of what would become the Reform Movement.
Needless to say, the establishment Jewish community was not
happy with this.

Today the building looks much as it did when it was

completed save for the reading desk having been moved
from the center to the east, just in front of the Ark.

The synagogue's Moorish style reflects the origins of the
congregation, which came from a Spanish and Portuguese
synagogue. The oil-lit Ner Tamid (Eternal Light) was designed
for the congregation and was made in 1848. Above the open
grille Ark is an organ that was completed at the same time as
the synagogue; the choir sits nearby behind the Ark.

The New West End Synagogue. St. Petersburgh
Place, W2. Tel: 020-7229-2335. Orthodox. Call for
service times. Tube: Queensway or Bayswater.

A mixture of Moorish, Gothic, Romanesque, and Byzantine
design, this 1879 structure was built by a congregation of
well-to-do families who needed a synagogue that was closer
to their homes near fashionable Kensington Gardens.

Ben Uri Art Society and Gallery. 126 Albert Street,
NW1. Tel: 020-7482-1234. Email: benuri@ort.org.
Hours: Monday–Thursday, 10 AM–5 PM; Sunday, 2 PM–5
PM during exhibitions. Closed Jewish holidays and bank
holidays. Tube: Camden Town.

Founded in 1915, this is a gallery of contemporary art and
also sponsors lectures and other programs. Its mission is to
promote Jewish art as part of Jewish cultural heritage.

The Jewish Museum—Camden Town. 129–131
Albert Street, NW1. Tel: 020-7284-1997.
Online: http://www.jewmusm.ort.org.
Tube: Camden Town.

Founded in 1932 and relocated to its new home in 1995,
London's Jewish Museum contains a number of temporary
and permanent exhibitions on Jewish life around the world.
It also sponsors educational programs.

The Jewish Museum, Camden.
Courtesy of the Jewish Museum, London

The history gallery tells the story of the Jews in Britain from their beginning and the artifacts on exhibit are very compelling. The ceremonial art gallery contains a number of Jewish ritual objects and includes a magnificent sixteenth-century Ark from an Italian synagogue. There are audio-visual programs as well as temporary exhibits and a bookshop.

The Finchley branch (see North London entry) contains the museum's social history collection and is well worth a visit.

The British Library, St. Pancras branch, Treasures Gallery. 96 Euston Road, NW1. Tel: 020-7412-7000. Hours: Monday, Wednesday, Thursday, Friday, 9:30 AM–

Silver Torah Scrolls, eighteenth century. *Courtesy of the Jewish Museum, London*

6 PM; Tuesday, 9:30 AM–8 PM; Saturday, 9:30 AM–5 PM; Sunday, 11:00 AM–5 PM. Tube: Warren Street.

In the Treasures Gallery is the Golden Haggadah, one of the finest Haggadah manuscripts that has survived from medieval Spain. The Haggadah, used on Passover during the Seder, commemorates the Israelites' exodus from Egypt. This one, believed to be from Barcelona circa 1320, contains splendid illuminations and French Gothic gold-tooled backgrounds, hence the Haggadah's name. The front of the book contains exquisite scenes from the Book of Exodus and in addition to the text, there are numerous Sephardic liturgical poems (piyyutim). The Haggadah is enclosed by an intricate seventeenth-century Italian binding, and as all Hebrew books, it is read from right to left. An electronic version, accompanied by audio and zooming aids, is found in the Turning the Pages room, which is accessible from the Treasures Gallery.

Kent House, Kensington. *Courtesy of Evelyn Friedlander*

The Spanish and Portuguese Synagogue.

Lauderdale Road, Maida Vale, W9. Tel: 020-7289-2573.
Tube: Maida Vale. From the tube stop, walk south on
Randolph Avenue, turn right on Sutherland Avenue. The
synagogue is at Lauderdale Road and Ashworth Road.

This is the heart of London's Sephardi Jewish community.
Davis and Emmanuel, the architects of the synagogue in
Upper Berkeley Street and the East London Synagogue in
Stepney, built this magnificent Sephardi synagogue in 1896.
It is a mixture of Gothic, Romanesque, and mock-Byzantine
elements and is typical of the late-Victorian era. The interior
is mostly wood and is no less grand than the exterior, but it
has an almost intimate feel nonetheless.

The New London Synagogue. 33 Abbey Rd, NW 8.
Tel: 020-7328-1026. Tube: St. John's Wood. From the
tube stop, walk north along Finchley Road (If you start
walking on Finchley, and it turns into Wellington Road,
you're going in the wrong direction.). Turn left into
Marlborough Place. The synagogue is at the corner of
Marlborough Place and Abbey Road.

Opened in 1882, the building's fairly plain exterior masks a
more ornate and lovely interior. Cast-iron columns and a
striking ceiling design make this late-Victorian synagogue
worth a visit—especially if you find yourself in the
neighborhood. The building had been sold in the 1960s and
was going to be torn down, but the developer who
purchased it liked it so much that he decided not to have it
destroyed. He sold it back to the congregation for the same
price that he had paid for it. The synagogue is a member of
the Assembly of Masorti Synagogues, which Americans will
recognize as following Conservative ritual.

The British Museum. Great Russell Street, WC1. Tube:
Tottenham Court Road, Russell Square, or Holborn.
Tel: 020-7323-8000. Online: www.britishmuseum.ac.uk.
Hours: Saturday–Wednesday, 10 AM–5:30 PM; Thursday
and Friday, 10 AM–8:30 PM. Admission: free, but donation
suggested. Special exhibitions may charge admission.

You can spend days here looking at all the loot from the former
British Empire. If you only get to one museum in London, this
one should be it. There is quite a bit of Jewish interest here—
check out the Ancient Palestine Room. And don't forget the
original Balfour Declaration in the Manuscript Room.

The National Portrait Gallery. St. Martin's Place, WC2.
Tube: Charing Cross, Leicester Square, Picadilly Circus,
or Embankment. Tel: 020-7306-0055.

Online: www.npg.org.uk. Hours: Monday–Saturday,
10 AM–6 PM; Sunday 12 Noon–6 PM. Admission: free, but
special exhibitions and lectures may charge admission.

Although there is no Jewish section, this visual gallery of
British history contains portraits of many Jewish figures—
Moses Montefiore, Israel Zangwill, and on and on.

Victoria and Albert Museum. Cromwell Road, SW7.
Tube: South Kensington. Tel: 020-7942-2000.
Online: www.vam.ac.uk. Hours: Monday–Sunday,
10 AM–5:45 PM. Admission: £5, free from 4:30–6 PM.

While this will not provide a respite from the hordes of
shoppers in Kensington, it will present you with a good
diversion—especially on a rainy day. The Victoria and
Albert Museum has a wonderful collection of Jewish ritual
objects.

Czech Memorial Scrolls Center. Kent House, Rutland
Gardens, SW7. Tel: 020-7584-3741. Hours: Tuesday
and Thursday, 10 AM–4 PM. Tube: Knightsbridge.

Get out at the Sloane Street exit, walk up to Knightsbridge,
and turn left. Rutland Gardens is on your left around where
Knightsbridge becomes Kensington Road. The gallery is
above the Westminster Synagogue.

This is quite a moving exhibition. This museum tells the
story of the 1964 rescue of 1,564 Torahs that had been
confiscated by the Germans during World War II. Found in a
railroad car, they were brought to England and given on
permanent loan to Jewish communities throughout the
world, who have restored them and now use them. Some of
the Torahs are exhibited along with Mappot (Torah binders)
and other Torah accoutrements, some dating back to the
eighteenth century. It's a good opportunity to see some of the

only remains of the lost Jewish towns of Bohemia and Moravia.

Imperial War Museum Holocaust Exhibition.
Lambeth Road, SE1. Tel: 020-7416-5320.
Email: mail@iwm.org.uk.;
Online: http://www.iwm.org.uk/lambeth/lambeth.htm.
Hours: Daily, 10 AM–6 PM. Tube: Lambeth North,
Elephant and Castle, or Waterloo. Admission £5.50,
adults; seniors, free.

The Imperial War Museum's new exhibit on the Holocaust makes it even more worthwhile, and rewarding, to visit.

Four years in the making, the Holocaust Exhibition uses historical material to tell the story of the Nazis' persecution of the Jews and other groups before and during the Second World War. The 1200-square-meter display covers two floors and brings to Britain for the first time rare and important objects, some from former concentration and extermination camp museums in Germany, Poland, and the Ukraine.[7] Programs include films, lectures, educational outreach programs, and a number of publications.

NORTH AND NORTHWEST LONDON

Stamford Hill

This is an area with a large Hasidic population.

AJEX Military Museum.
AJEX House, East Bank, Stamford Hill. Tel: 020-8800-2844. Call for hours. Tube: Manor House.

A long walk from the tube—take Seven Sisters Road to Amherst Park and make a right until you reach East Bank.

This small museum houses a display of Jewish books, photos, and other memorabilia from the eighteenth century to the present.

Finchley

The Jewish Museum—Finchley. 80 East End Road, N3. Tel: 020-8349-1143.
Online: http://www.jewmusm.ort.org. Hours: Monday–Thursday, 10:30 AM–5 PM; Sunday, 10:30 AM–4:30 PM. Closed Sundays in August, Jewish holidays, public holidays, and bank holiday weekends. Tube: Finchley Central.

From the tube, make a right onto Station Road and then a left onto Regents Park Road. Follow Regents Park Road to East End Road and make a left. It's a very long walk, but a five-minute taxi ride if you can get one.

Located in the massive Sternberg Centre, this branch of the museum houses exhibitions both permanent and temporary about the history of Jewish immigration in London, including various reconstructions of Jewish life in the East End. The museum also presents lectures and educational programs, and conducts what are, in my opinion, the best guided walks of the old Jewish East End. Call for information.

The Sternberg Centre for Judaism. 80 East End Road, Finchley, N3. Tel: 020-8343-0901. Tube: Finchley Central.

A number of Jewish educational and other institutions have their offices here and the facilities include a synagogue

(British Reform), a mikvah, an excellent bookstore devoted to Jewish subjects, a Holocaust Memorial Garden, and a biblical garden. Call for information.

LONDON RESOURCES

Board of Deputies of British Jews has a Jewish community information line: Tel: 020-7543-5421.

Synagogues

There are so many synagogues in London that it would be best to call one of the administrative offices to find one that meets your needs. Call these same organizations for the location and phone number of a mikvah.

United Synagogue—Orthodox. Tel: 020-8343-8989.

Federation of Synagogues—Orthodox. Tel: 020-8202-2263.

Union of Orthodox Hebrew Congregations—Orthodox and various Hasidic groups (Belz, Satmar, Gur, Square, Sanz Klausenberg, Lubavitch, Bobov—the ganse mishpocha). Tel: 020-8802-6226.

Masorti—Conservative. Tel: 020-8201-8772. Online: http://www.masorti.org.uk.

Reform (similar to American Conservative). Tel: 020-8349-4731.

Liberal and Progressive (similar to American Reform). Tel: 020-7580-1663.

Sephardic—Spanish and Portuguese Jews' Congregations. Tel: 020-7289-2573.

Banner of the London Jewish Bakers Union. *Courtesy of the Jewish Museum, London*

Kosher Food

The four main supervising authorities in London are the **London Beth Din, Kedassia**, the **Federation Kashrus Board**, and the **Sephardi Kashrus Authority**. The Beth Din is run by United Synagogue, Kedassia by the Union of Orthodox Hebrew Congregations, Federation by the Federation of Synagogues, an Orthodox group, and the Sephardi Kashrus Authority by the Sephardic Synagogues.

West, Central, and Near Central London

Unfortunately, the pickings in Central London are pretty slim. Most of the kosher restaurants, take-out (called "take-away" in England), bakeries, are in the northern districts of Golders Green, Hendon, Finchley, or in those suburbs with large Jewish populations such as Edgeware and Ilford.

Restaurants

The Munch Box. 41 Greville Street, EC1.
Tel: 020-7242-5487. Tube: Chancery Lane. Prepared
foods. Beth Din.

Macabi King of Falafel. 59 Wentworth Street, E1.
Tel: 020-7247-6660. Tube: Aldgate or Aldgate East.
Federation Beth Din.

As you can tell from the name, falafel is the specialty.

Café Hillel. B'nai B'rith Hillel Foundation, 1–2
Endsleigh Street, WC1. Tel: 020-7388-0801.
Tube: Euston Square. Beth Din.
Hours: Monday–Thursday, noon–2:30 PM.

Friday night Shabbat meals available if booked and paid for
in advance by Thursday at 11 AM. Open sporadic hours
during the summer, as this is primarily a student restaurant.

Reubens. 79 Baker Street, W1. Tel: 020-7486-0035.
Sephardi Kashrus Authority. Meat. Tube: Baker Street.
Hours: Sunday–Thursday, 11:30 AM–3:45 PM,
5 PM–10 PM; Friday, 11:30 AM–1 PM. Closed Saturday.

Reuben's serves a varied menu of traditional Jewish food,
English-style deli, and Israeli items.

Six 13. 19 Wigmore Street, W1. Tel: 020-7629-6133.
Beth Din. Meat. Tube: Bond Street.
Hours: Monday–Thursday, noon–3 PM, 4:30–10:45 PM;
Friday, noon–1 PM; Saturday, after Shabbat; Sunday,
noon–3, 6–9 PM. Reservations recommended.

This welcome addition to the limited kosher dining
options in Central London describes its cuisine as kosher
fusion. The eclectic menu features appetizers from salads

to smoked salmon to foie gras with caramelized apples and entrees such as steak, grilled chicken with noodles, chili, spring onions, bok choy and coriander, and English staples such as roast beef with Yorkshire pudding. Omelettes and fish are also available. Desserts run the gamut from apple pie and raspberry tart to chocolate truffles and sorbets. Two- and three-course lunch is served from noon to 3 PM and a pretheater menu is served from 5:30 to 7 PM.

Take-out and Groceries

The pickings, again, are slim, but here are some reliable options.

Selfridges Department Store, Oxford Street. Tube: Bond Street or Marble Arch.

There is a kosher food counter in the Selfridges' food halls on the mezzanine just up from the ground floor. They sell prepared foods, packaged and canned foods, sandwiches, and candy. Each item carries a different hashgacha and the prepared foods are made by a number of companies that are supervised by the Beth Din. This is really a great find.

Supermarkets and the supermarket sections of the large department stores have terrific produce sections where you can make your own fresh salads to take out. You can also buy items such as canned fish and hard-boiled eggs. Best to stay away from the bread unless it is marked kosher.

North and Northwest London
Restaurants Near Golders Green. Tube: Golders Green.

If you turn right when you leave the tube station and walk along Golders Green Road for a couple of blocks, you will come to several kosher restaurants, bakeries, and take-out places. Here are some to try.

Bloom's. 130 Golders Green Road, NW11. Tel: 020-8455-1338, 3033. Beth Din. Meat. Hours: until 1 AM Sunday–Thursday. Open for lunch only on Friday. Saturday from one hour after Shabbat until 4 AM. Reserve.

A famous London kosher eatery with classic Eastern European fare. This is the second outlet of a restaurant that for decades stood in London's East End on Whitechapel Road—but the original Bloom's morphed into a Burger King a few years ago.

Café on the Green. 122 Golders Green Road, NW11. Tel: 020-8209-0232. Dairy. Cholov Yisrael, Beth Din. Daily and after Shabbat in winter.

Tasty Pizza. 252 Golders Green Road, NW11. Tel: 020-8209-0023. Beth Din; Kedassia. Pizza.

Milk & Honey. 124 Golders Green Road, NW11. Tel: 020-8455-0664. Kedassia. Dairy and vegetarian. Take-out available.

Solly's. 148a Golders Green Road, NW11. Tel: 020-8455-0004. Beth Din. Meat.

Restaurants in Hendon

Kaifeng. 51 Church Road, NW4. Tel: 020-8203-7888. Online: http://www.kaifeng.co.uk. Beth Din. Meat/Chinese. Restaurant, take-out, they will deliver to your hotel. Tube: Hendon Central.

Folman's. 134 Brent Street, NW4. Tel: 020-8202-5592. Federation. Dairy. Tube: Hendon Central.

CHAPTER THREE

The West Country

Exeter

An important Jewish center prior to the Expulsion, Exeter now has only one hundred fifty Jews. The present community was founded in the early-eighteenth century. Although its numbers decreased dramatically in the nineteenth century, there is some evidence that it is today undergoing a revival.

The medieval community probably lived on High Street and local records mention Jewish-owned business transactions dating back to 1181. The Jewish community here flourished, and in addition to a synagogue, it had its own cemetery.

In the thirteenth century, there was an increase in anti-Jewish hostility on the part of the clergy and the local residents. In 1287, the Synod of Exeter promulgated a number of anti-Jewish laws just prior to the Expulsion from the entire realm in 1290.

SIGHTS

Synagogue. Synagogue Place, Mary Arches Street.
Tel: 01392-251529.
Online http://exetersynagogue.org.uk. Call for
information about visits and services.

The interior is done in dark wood with the exception of the Ark, which is wood but constructed with marble fittings and supports.

Abraham Ezekiel and Kitty Jacobs acquired the land on which the synagogue was built in 1763 and the synagogue was consecrated in 1764.

The building underwent refurbishing in 1835, 1854, and 1905. Heavily damaged during World War II, there was an extensive reconstruction in 1980 of the entire first floor. Assistance from English Heritage (a governmental organization) provided for a further restoration in 1998 of the historic Ark along with some of the walls. English Heritage also provided funds for the installation of central heating.

Over the years, the synagogue has been a center of Jewish community life in Devon and a significant contributor to Devon life in general as well as to that of the rest of England. In 1815, a service was held to benefit the Devon and Exeter Hospital; in 1821, a special service celebrated the coronation of King George IV; and in 1862, a memorial service mourned the death of Prince Albert, husband of Queen Victoria.

In 1980, the synagogue once again began to hold regular services, which now take place twice a month, on Rosh Hashanah and Yom Kippur, and on several other holidays. There is a community Seder on Passover.

Cemetery. Magdalen Street. For information and visits, contact the Synagogue. Tel: 01392-251529.

In 1757, the Jews' Burial Ground was established just outside the city's Roman wall. Jewish tradition dictates that a place to bury the dead has priority over a synagogue as communal prayer doesn't require a special building. The ninety-nine-year lease bears the name of "Abraham Ezekiel of the parish of St Kerrian in the city of Exon, silversmith". The fee for the land was five shillings and the original plot was 80 feet by 22 feet. The lease required Abraham Ezekiel to surround the burial ground with an 8-foot-high brick, stone, or cob wall.

Additional land was acquired adjacent to the cemetery in 1803 and a new lease was issued to Moses Mordecai, also a silversmith. Land was added a few more times in the next century and a half.

By 1951, all the leases had expired, though nobody took any note of it. But as a result, legal difficulties arose when the city of Exeter wanted to build a roadway that required the purchase of the cemetery and the exhumation of all the graves. The roadway project was abandoned for reasons having nothing to do with the cemetery, but the issue made the congregation aware that it no longer owned the land. In 1977, the cemetery was purchased outright on behalf of the congregation.

Repairs were made to the walls and the chapel in the 1980s and the cemetery was fitted with new gates. Some burials still take place here, but the congregation uses another cemetery in Exwick provided by the Exeter City Council.

Plymouth

THE CITY OF Plymouth is the home of the oldest Ashkenazi synagogue in the English-speaking world. Located in Catherine Street, next to the Guildhall, the building was completed in 1762, two years prior to the synagogue in Exeter. The site was next to a spring that was used as a mikvah.

SIGHTS

Synagogue: Synagogue Chambers.
Tel: 01752-301955. For visits and services, call the president of the congregation, Mr. Benny Greenberg, 01752-773309.
Online http://www.plymouthsynagogue.co.uk

Built in the Georgian style, it has a plain brick exterior, a pitched roof, and semicircular windows. There have been some interior changes, but for the most part the synagogue looks a good deal as it did when it was built in 1762.

Inside, the Baroque Ark has some nice examples of shadow painting. The women's gallery, which was originally opposite the synagogue's western wall, was enlarged in 1807 and the cast-iron columns you see today were added along with the painted latticework. Children's seats were added to the back of the gallery in 1811, and it was enlarged again in the middle of the nineteenth century. The lighting has been changed over the decades from the original brass candelabras to the electric fixtures you see today. The wooden pine benches are original pieces and the windows are twentieth century.

CHAPTER FOUR

The Midlands

Birmingham

Birmingham, in the part of England known as West Midlands, was a large regional manufacturing center and as such it attracted some of the first Jewish settlers in the English provinces. One of the oldest Jewish communities in the provinces, it dates back to 1730 and perhaps even a little earlier.

The early Jewish settlers, primarily peddlers, used the city as a base from which to travel to other parts of the region during the week. They would return to their homes in the city for Shabbat.

The earliest Jewish institution in Birmingham was a cemetery in 1730, and records indicate the first synagogue was established in 1780 in the area known as the Froggery.

Today Birmingham has about three thousand Jews and a number of institutions that support the community.

SIGHTS

Singer's Hill Synagogue, Birmingham Hebrew Congregation. Ellis Street, B1 1HL.
Tel: 0121-643-0884. Shabbat services at this historic shul are at 10 AM. Call ahead for details.

The oldest congregation in Birmingham, the building was consecrated in 1856 by England's Chief Rabbi, Dr. Adler. The architect, H. Yeoville Thompson, also designed the City Council House and Art Gallery.

Singer's Hill Synagogue contains several huge, ornate chandeliers. Though the stained glass, which depicts Biblical events, is in the same style, it was actually added later.

In addition to the main sanctuary, there is a smaller room, known as the Children's Synagogue. A smaller version of the main shul, it is used for daily services.

During the summer, the synagogue holds a civic service for visitors that includes prayers and readings in English. Call for details.

RESOURCES

Synagogues

Singer's Hill Synagogue, Birmingham Hebrew Congregation. Ellis Street, B1 1HL.
Tel: 0121-643-0884.

Central Synagogue. 133 Pershore Road.
Tel: 0121-440-4044.

Tourist Information

Israel Information Centre, Bookshop, and Reference Library. Singer's Hill, Blucher Street.
Tel: 0121-643-2688.
Email: rjacobs@iicmids.u-net.com.

Kosher Food

A. Gee. 75 Pershore Road, Tel: 0121-440-2160.
Deli, bakery, butcher.

For additional information on kosher food, Call the Singer's Hill Synagogue, 0121-643-0884

Mikvah

There is a mikvah at the Central Synagogue.
Tel: 0121-440-5853. Call for appointments.

Lincoln

THERE IS ONLY a very small Jewish community today in Lincoln, but the city figures prominently in English Jewish history—although several of its chapters are sad. It is one of the few places where you can see sights from before the Expulsion in 1290. Examples of Jewish buildings from the Middle Ages still exist in what was known as the Jewry.

In the Middle Ages, the Jews of Lincoln were nearly equal in importance to those of London. Lincoln, a center of Jewish business, was home to Aaron of Lincoln, a prominent financier. Lincoln was also home to well-known Jewish scholars, including the Tosafist Rabbi Berachiah of Nicole (a.k.a. Benedict of Lincoln).

The Tosafists

The Tosafists were students, sons, and sons-in-law of RASHI (Rabbi Shlomo Yitzchaki—1040–1105), the rabbi from Troyes, France who wrote extensive and laboriously detailed explanations and analyses (known as commentaries) of the text of the Torah and the Talmud, including a grammar with which they could be studied. This was revolutionary in its day because up to that point, none of these study devices had been written down.

The Tosafists continued Rashi's work by commenting on his commentaries. The Hebrew word "tosafot" means additions, and Rashi's followers used Rashi's own work as a point of departure for such additional analysis so that it would become the standard for the study of Torah and Talmud within their own schools of rabbinic study.

What made the work of the Tosafists so revolutionary was that through it, Jewish scholars had, for the first time, a logical method of studying Rashi, and through a process of questioning, analyzing, and comparing his writings, gained greater access to the Torah and the Talmud. As a result, they were able to make new interpretations of Jewish law, and to existing interpretations, refine or rethink conclusions to problems arising from its legal texts, and could themselves provide the impetus for further work in future generations.

In March 1190, Lincoln's Jews were attacked by Crusaders who had been rampaging through the countryside (see also chapter 10). They escaped significant harm under the protection of the local sheriff and Lincoln's Bishop, "Saint" Hugh.

But the story of the boy who would become known as "Little Saint Hugh" is very different. In the spring of 1255, some time around Passover, the body of a young boy, Hugh, was found in the well of Lincoln's Jewish quarter. As the well was near the house of a Jew named Copin, he was questioned and tortured and was alleged to have admitted killing the boy to obtain his blood for use in Jewish ceremonies. Copin was executed and nearly one hundred Jews were tried in London as accomplices—eighteen were executed.

Looked upon as a saint, but never actually beatified by the Roman Catholic Church, Little Hugh was credited with the performance of miracles. His tomb, under Lincoln's cathedral, was an elaborate one that became a destination for pilgrims up until the Reformation.

The so-called martyrdom of Little Hugh is mentioned in Chaucer's "The Prioress's Tale" and was also the subject of ballads in England and France.

The Jewish quarter came under siege yet again eleven years later when the so-called Disinherited Knights, under the leadership of Simon de Montfort, destroyed the synagogue and burned the Jewish debt records. By the time of the Expulsion in 1290, the community's assets had become property of the Crown.

There was a small, short-lived community here again in the early-nineteenth century and during World War II, when evacuees from London were sent to Lincoln.

SIGHTS

Jew's House and Jew's Court. 2–3 Steep Hill.

Aaron the Jew's House. 47 Steep Hill, built in 1170.

Among the medieval houses that line the cobbled street of

Steep Hill are two buildings believed to have been built and owned by Jews. Aaron of Lincoln, the presumed owner of the building at 47 Steep Hill, was one of the most important financiers in England and second in wealth only to King Henry II. Both buildings have withstood not only the ravages of time but also several anti-Jewish riots.

Norwich

THIS SMALL NORFOLK community of less than two hundred Jews has the unfortunate distinction of living in the city that gave Europe its first recorded blood libel (see chapter 1), when Jews were accused of killing young William of Norwich in 1144. But large-scale attacks didn't occur until nearly one hundred years later, in the 1230s, when Jews were accused of kidnapping and forcing the circumcision of a Christian child.

Until 1260, Norwich's Jewish community of between one hundred and one hundred fifty was home to a number of scholars, some of whose works are in the Vatican archives. Its financiers did business with local nobles and tradespeople. By the time of the Expulsion of 1290, only about fifty Jews lived here.

Jews did not settle in Norwich again until the beginning of the eighteenth century. The community bought a cemetery in 1813 and built a synagogue in 1828. Unfortunately, that building was destroyed by German bombs during World War II, but it was rebuilt in 1948.

SIGHTS

The Music House (a.k.a. **Jurnet's House**). Wensum
Lodge, King Street.

The origins of this flint house are uncertain, but it is
believed to have been built in 1175 by a Jew named Jurnet.
The Jews of Norwich lived in the vicinity of White Lion
Street and in the Haymarket district. Isaac, Jurnet's son, was
a very wealthy financier.

Norwich Cathedral, the Close. Tel: 01603-764-385.
Open daily 7:30 AM–6 PM (until 7 PM mid-May to mid-
September). Donation suggested.

This imposing Norman building is located in England's
largest close—an enclosed space usually surrounding a
church or cathedral. The cathedral is made of flint rubble,
and the facing is limestone ashlar. Begun in 1096, the
cathedral was almost complete by 1145, and the interior
floor plan is virtually unchanged from that time.

In 1144, the remains of William of Norwich (see chapter
1) were brought to the cathedral for reburial following his
murder. William's murder was Europe's first documented
charge of blood libel or ritual murder against Jews, and the
body was brought to the cathedral in the hope that a cult
would be established in his name. Apart from the anti-
Jewish reasons for such a cult, there were some other
practical ones—cults at various churches were a source of
income from pilgrims.

Today, William's burial site is the Chapel of the Holy
Innocents (dedicated in 1997), located near the choir screen.
It commemorated "the sufferings of all innocent victims"
according to the cathedral's literature. Although the
literature does make general reference to anti-Jewish

sentiment surrounding William's murder, it doesn't mention the blood libel. The cathedral has set aside this spot as a "place of prayer for reconciliation between people of different faiths, remembering especially all victims of Christian–Jewish persecution." Presumably, they mean Christian persecution of Jews.

RESOURCES

Norwich Hebrew Congregation. 3a Earlham Road. Tel: 01603-623948. To reach the secretary, call 01603-506482.

CHAPTER FIVE

The North West

Liverpool

I DON'T KNOW about you, but Liverpool is forever connected in my mind with John Lennon, Paul McCartney, Ringo Starr, and George Harrison—the Beatles. They're not Jewish, but who cares!

This vibrant Jewish community in this famous seaport city dates back to the eighteenth century and today numbers about 3,000 individuals. Records and maps from that time show a synagogue off of Stanley Street. The first cemetery was consecrated in 1789 and later, in 1808, another synagogue was built in Seel Street. The Princes Road Synagogue was built in 1874 and is today what the British call a "listed building"—a national land-mark.

In the mid-nineteenth century, Liverpool's 3,000-strong Jewish community was the second largest in England and its numbers were enhanced by Russian and Polish refugees at the end of that century. The Ashkenazi Jews lived side by side with a Sephardic community that was here for a short time from 1892 to 1914.

Relations between Jews and the non-Jewish population have been good and Liverpool had its first Jewish Lord Mayor in 1863—Charles Mozley. Since then four other Jews have occu-pied the office.

By the 1970s, the Jewish population had grown to 7,500, but it has dropped considerably since then, even in the last ten years. Some 4,000 Jews lived here in the mid-1990s.

Liverpool's Jews have a solid nucleus of community organi-zations that include schools, charitable societies, and a yeshiva—some of those organizations go back to the early-nine-teenth century. Liverpool is also the home of Britain's first Hebrew day school.

SIGHTS

Old Hebrew Congregation. Princes Road, L8.
Tel: 0151-709-3431.

> The congregation here was founded in 1740 and the synagogue was consecrated in 1874.

RESOURCES

Merseyside Jewish Representative Council.
433 Smithdown Road, L15 3JL. Tel: 0151-733-2292.
Synagogue and kosher food information.

Bookshop

Youth and Community Center. Harold House,
Dunbabin Road. Open Sundays only.
Tel: 0151-475-5825

Manchester

T HERE ARE SOME 27,000 Jews in this northern industrial city. The second-largest Jewish community in
England, it dates back to the late-eighteenth century when the
Nathan brothers, Lemon and Jacob of Liverpool, founded the
first synagogue. Some of Manchester's earliest Jews included
Nathan Mayer Rothschild, who began his cotton exporting business there. By the early-nineteenth century, a cemetery had been
established, along with the Manchester Jewish Philanthropic
Society. The congregation moved into what would be its home
for more than one hundred years in 1858.

The first congregation, which was what we would define
today as Orthodox, was joined in 1856 by a Reform congregation (see chapter 1), as the result of a community disagreement.

Jewish merchants from Central Europe arrived beginning in
the mid-nineteenth century, and refugee Romanian Jews in
1869 and young Jewish conscripts fleeing the Russian Czar's

armies followed them in the 1870s. Jews from the Middle East and North Africa joined the European Jews at about the same time. And, as was true in other British cities, the refugees from Russian pogroms arrived between 1881 and 1914.

Many Jews were involved in the textile industry and Manchester was home to large numbers of Jewish clothing manufacturers in addition to the usual tailors and used clothing merchants. Indeed, a significant innovation of that industry was pioneered by Jewish manufacturers—waterproof clothing. More modern methods have been developed in recent years, but for generations Jews dominated this sector of the clothing industry.

Manchester has numerous community organizations and synagogues and though its population has declined in recent years, it is again on the upswing as it draws Jews from London. Many live in the suburbs of Cheshire and Salford. Among the city's most noted residents was Chaim Weizmann, Israel's first president, who lived in Manchester from 1904 to 1916.

The traditional Jewish neighborhood was located in Cheetham Hill, but most Jews now live in the suburbs of Salford, Chesire, and Prestwich.

SIGHTS

The Manchester Jewish Museum. 190 Cheetham Hill Road. Tel: 0161-834-9879; 832-7353.
Hours: Monday–Thursday, 10:30 AM–4 PM;
Sunday 10:30 AM–5 PM. Admission: £3.50
adults, £8.50 families. Metrolink: Victoria. Buses: 21, 56, 59, 89, 134, 135, 167.

Situated in the old Spanish and Portuguese synagogue built in 1873, the museum now houses both permanent and temporary exhibitions about Manchester and British Jewry. The recordings of the oral history project are particularly compelling. They also offer a good calendar of talks and other events by local historians and experts. This is the place to call for a walking tour of Manchester's Jewish neighborhoods.

Prestwich Village Cemetery. For information on visits, contact the Manchester branch of the Jewish Historical Society; tel: 0161-740-6403.

Acquired in 1841 by the congregation that became the Great Synagogue, this badly neglected site constitutes the oldest extant burial ground of Manchester Jewry. Cleared of weeds in winter 1999–2000, it is still in need of attention.[8]

MANCHESTER RESOURCES

Synagogues

Manchester has dozens of synagogues in various areas. It's best to call the **Jewish Representative Council** for information; tel: 0161-720-8721.

Kosher Food

Kosher information: Manchester Beth Din; tel: 0161-740-9711.

Hyman's Deli. 41 Wilmstow Road, Cheadle. Tel: 0161-491-1100. Beth Din.

State Fayre Groceries. 77 Middleton Road, Manchester. Tel: 0161-740-3435. Beth Din.

Antonio's. Bury Road and Park Road (in Jewish community center). Tel: 0161-795-8911. Beth Din.

PRESTWICH RESOURCES

Kosher Food

Deli King. Kings Road. Tel: 0161-798-7370. Beth Din.

Haber's. 8 Kings Road. Tel: 0161-773-2046. Beth Din.

Jehu Deli. 5 Parkhill. Tel: 0161-740-2816. Beth Din.

J. S. Kosher Restaurant. 7 Kings Road. Tel: 0161-798-7776. Beth Din. Meat.

Bookstores

B. Horwitz. 20 King Edwards Building, Bury Road. Tel: 0161-740-5897.

B. Horwitz Judaica World. 2 Kings Road. Tel: 0161-773-4956. Email: melachim11@aol.com.

Mikvah

Manchester and District Mikva. Sedgley Park Road. Tel: 0161-773-1537.

SALFORD RESOURCES

Kosher Food

S. Halpern Grocery. 59 Leicester Road. Tel: 0161-792-1752. Beth Din.

Kosher Hotel

Fulda's Hotel. 144 Old Bury Road.
Tel: 0161-740-4748.
Online: http://www.fuldashotel.com. Beth Din.

Glatt kosher and in the middle of this large Orthodox Jewish
community. Easy walk to synagogue.

Mikvah

Manchester Communal Mikvah. Broome Holme,
Tetlow Lane. Tel: 0161-792-3970. For Friday night and
yom tov appointments, call 0161-740-4071, or
0161-740-5199.

CHAPTER SIX

The North East

York

THE TINY JEWISH community of York, comprised of some twenty-five persons, is heir to the most gruesome episode in the history of the relationship between England and the Jewish people.

Clifford's Tower, now rebuilt on the same site as the medieval castle keep in which the atrocity occurred, still stands, a monument now to the memory.

The existence of a royal castle in York, and the financial needs of the local nobility and clergy, had led to the growth of a Jewish community here in the Middle Ages. The use of Jewish financing for a whole array of projects was nothing new—indeed, the Crown itself regularly availed itself of those services, and the Jewish congregation generated significant revenue for the Crown.

In March 1190, on Shabbat Hagadol, the Sabbath just before Passover, the nobles, clergy, and the populace of York, incited by the fervor of the Crusades, began setting fire to and looting Jewish homes. Frightened, the Jews all fled to the castle for shelter. A mob led by a monk, and by local officials who were indebted to Jewish moneylenders, raged outside—their shouts and jeers made it clear what fate awaited the Jews. When a stone fell from the castle and killed the monk, the mob's ire was inflamed even more.

Low on food and painfully aware of the fate that awaited them—either torture and death or forced baptism—many chose to follow Rabbi Yom Tov of Joigny, their leader, and take their own lives by setting fire to the castle. By dawn the mob had captured the burning building and massacred the Jews who were still left alive. Their rage still not exhausted, the mob went to the cathedral and burned all the Jewish debt records. Finally, they moved on to other towns. History records that massacres and expulsions of Jews took place in many places at this same time, including Lincoln, Bury St. Edmonds, and Leicester.

This and other instances of the destruction of Jewish debt records led to the formation of the Exchequer of the Jews (see chapter 1).

SIGHTS

Clifford's Tower. York Castle. Off Tower Street.

York Castle and the tower were badly damaged in the massacre and the fire. Repairs were made between 1190 and 1194 and the mound on which the tower sits was raised. The present tower actually dates from the middle of the thirteenth century. During excavations in the beginning of the twentieth century, burned timber from the massacre was found several feet beneath the mound.

In 1978, a plaque was dedicated at the tower memorializing the massacred Jews.

York Minister. College Street. Tel: 01904-557-216. Hours: Daily 12 Noon–6 PM. Call for changes. Online: http://www.yorkminster.org. No visitors will be permitted inside on Sundays until 1 PM. Donations suggested.

One of the windows in York Minister's chapter house (vestibule CHs6) contains a statue of Synagoga—a blindfolded woman with a falling crown and broken banner. There is another one, which originally stood in the chapter house until 1798, on display in the Minster.

Note: The pair of statues known as Ecclesia and Synagoga, or Church and Synagogue, fairly common in continental Europe, particularly France and Germany, are not common in England. Seen as statues and also as paintings, they represent the religious conflict between Judaism and Christianity, and they always have common characteristics—two women: one beautiful, well dressed, smiling, with a halo or crown represents the Church; the other, Judaism, is disheveled, her head bowed, she is usually blindfolded, wearing an askew crown of thorns and holding a broken staff, a serpentine staff, or broken pieces of the Ten Commandments.

RESOURCES

York Hebrew Congregation. 3 Rawcliffe Grove, YO3 4NR. Tel: 01904-624479. Direct inquiries to B. Sugar.

CHAPTER SEVEN

Wales

WALES'S SMALL JEWISH community lives primarily in the seaport city of Cardiff, but that isn't the country's oldest Jewish settlement.

Jews were expelled from Wales in 1290 with the rest of the Jews in Britain, but in the eighteenth century they began to return. Prior to the Expulsion, there were individual Jews living in places like Caerleon and Chepstow, but Wales was not a hospitable place for Jews, and regions of the country were legally permitted to deny Jews residence.

In 1731, records show that Jews lived in the industrial seaport city of Swansea and that they organized a community in 1768. The year 1840 saw the establishment of a Jewish community in Cardiff.

The Jewish population of Wales rose with the immigration of Russian Jews following the pogroms of the late-nineteenth and early-twentieth centuries, and the new immigrants found a market for the services of pawnbrokers in the many mining towns of the country. As might have been expected, given the historical animosity toward Jewish moneylenders, there was a fair amount of resentment on the part of the miners, and anti-Jewish riots were a component of the 1911 miners' strikes. Jews moved to other places as a result. After World War I, the Jewish communities in the mining towns disappeared.

In 2000, some Jews called Wales home. Of those, 1,200 lived in Cardiff, and 245 lived in Swansea. There were about 10 Jews in the town of Newport and just under 50 in Llandudno and Colwyn Bay.

Resources

CARDIFF

Synagogues

Penylan Synagogue (Orthodox). Brandreth Road. Tel: 029-20473728.

New Synagogue (British Reform). Moira Terrace. Tel: 029-20491689.

Kosher Food

Contact Rabbi Levey at the Penylan Synagogue, Brandreth Road. Tel: 029-20473728.

LLANDUDNO

Synagogue: 28 Church Walks. Tel: 01492-572549.

NEWPORT

Synagogue: 45 St. Marks Crescent.
Tel: 01633-262308. The synagogue was built
in 1871.

SWANSEA

Hebrew Congregation, Fyfnone. Tel: 01792-401205.
Call for directions, times of services, and other
information.

CHAPTER EIGHT

Scotland

*I*F YOU'VE NEVER been to Scotland, your most vivid images of the country may very well be from the film version of the Broadway musical *Brigadoon*, written, as it happens, by two American Jews, Alan Jay Lerner and Frederick Loewe. And though *Brigadoon* is the product of a colorful imagination, not to mention the creativity of MGM's set designers, Scotland is real, and the country makes for a wonderful vacation filled with spectacular scenery and warm, friendly people. But to see the few Jewish sights in the country, you will have to head not to the Highlands but to its cities—primarily Glasgow and Edinburgh.

Scotland's small Jewish community (roughly 7,000 and dwindling) was established at the end of the eighteenth and the beginning of the nineteenth centuries when a small congregation was formed in Edinburgh in 1780. Although it didn't last very long, another grew up in 1816. A Jewish community was founded in Glasgow in 1823, and before long it became the larger of the two. But it is interesting to note that the city of Aberdeen's Marischal College was one of the first British universities to give a degree to a Jew—Jacob de Castro Sarmento—in 1739.[9]

The Russian pogroms of the 1880s to the early-1900s drove many Eastern European Jews from their homes and brought some to England and also to Scotland. To be sure, the primary destination for most was New York City and other places in America, but a large number of British Jews, including most of Scotland's, can trace their beginnings as citizens of Great Britain back to those immigrations. Stories are told of unscrupulous ship captains discharging refugees on Scotland's shores and telling them that they were in New York. But that duplicity proved to be a blessing because Jews in Scotland, which is almost devoid of anti-Semitism, have thrived and have become an integral part of its social, political, scientific, and cultural life.

In those early days, Jews earned a living in traditional Jewish occupations—tailoring, shoemaking, engaging in small-time commerce, and, of course, peddling. The peddlers were the ones who made their way to the Highlands—those often bleak but compelling northern regions of the country that are the stuff of story and legend. As has been the case in most countries, the Jews of Scotland developed their own language—a Scots-Yiddish. But today there are only a handful of Jews in the cities and towns of the Highlands.

Glasgow

ISAAC COHEN WAS the first Jew to settle in the south-west city of Glasgow in 1812. He was just one of a hand-ful of Jews—twenty years later, there were only forty-seven Jews in the city. With such a small group, the Jews met for prayer at the home of the shochet (ritual slaughterer), Moses Lisenheim.

In 1835 the first cemetery was established, but it fell into disuse in 1851. By 1842 there were enough Jews in town to foster a dispute intense enough for the congregation to split. At the time, services were held in a hall leased from Glasgow's medical school, and because dissections were performed there, some found it an inappropriate place to pray.

Some two hundred Jews lived in Glasgow in 1850, and in 1858 the Glasgow Hebrew Congregation was established. The synagogue in Garnethill was built in 1879 and stands today as the city's only Jewish landmark.

Glasgow's Jewish population was enlarged by refugees from the Russian pogroms in 1881, and by 1897, some 4,000 Jews lived in the city; there were 6,500 by 1902. The immigrants, mostly tailors and shoemakers, settled in the slum district known as the "Gorbals." The author Ralph Glasser recounts life in the district in his *Growing Up in the Gorbals* (Chatto and Windus, London, 1989).

Today the Gorbals is long gone and Glasgow's Jewish popu-lation has prospered and moved to the suburbs. Though rela-tively small in number (about 6,500), Glasgow Jewry is active in community causes and Israel-centered philanthropy. To find out about Jewish events in town, look through the *Jewish Echo* and *Israel Today*.

SIGHTS

Garnethill Synagogue. 125/7 Hill Street, G3.
Tel: 0141-332-4151.

> This lovely Victorian synagogue built in 1879 is now also the home of the Scottish Jewish Archives.

Queen's Park Synagogue. Falloch Road.
Tel: 0141-632-2139. Some beautiful stained glass windows depicting Jewish holidays are here.

For visits contact the Jewish Representative Council.

GLASGOW CEMETERIES[10]

Craigton Cemetery.

> This private cemetery contains a Jewish section, opened in 1880, but because it is so overgrown, no one has been able to locate it.

Janefield, the Western Necropolis, and Riddrie.

> Jewish sections were opened here in 1853, 1886, and 1908 respectively, but although they are maintained by the Jewish community or the Glasgow City Council, they have been heavily vandalized.

Glasgow Necropolis, Cathedral SQ. 1883.

This cemetery contains a façade of Jews' section.

RESOURCES

General Information

Jewish Representative Council. 222 Fenwick Road, Giffnock, G46 6UE. Tel: 0141-577-8228; E-mail: glasgow@ort.org.

Synagogues

Garnethill Synagogue. 125/7 Hill Street, G3. Tel: 0141-332-4151. Orthodox.

For additional synagogue information, contact the Jewish Representative Council (See above).

Kosher Food

Michael Morrison and Son. 52 Sinclair Drive, G42 9PY. Tel: 0141-632-0998. Not under official supervision.

Kaye's Restaurant. Maccabi Youth Center, May Terrace. Tel: 0141-620-3233.

Giffnock Kosher Deli. 200 Fenwick Road, Giffnock. Tel: 0141-638-8267.

Marlene's Kosher Deli. 2 Burnfield Road, Giffnock. Tel: 0141-638-4383.

Kosher Hotels

Forres Guest House. 10 Forres Avenue, Giffnock.
Tel: 0141-638-5554; E-mail: june.d@ukonline.co.uk.

Mikvah

Giffnock and Newlands Synagogue. Maryville
Avenue, Giffnock. Tel: 0141-620-3156.
Contact Mrs. C. Fletcher.

Bookstores

J & E Livingstone. 47/55 Sinclair Drive.
Tel: 0141-649-2962.

Edinburgh

TODAY THERE ARE only about 500 Jews in Edinburgh, Scotland's capital city. That number is down from the roughly 1,100 Jews who lived here in the late 1960s.

The congregation dates from 1816 and grew slowly from the founding twenty families. The immigration of Jewish refugees from Russia and Poland as the result of the pogroms of the late-nineteenth and early-twentieth centuries expanded the community, but it never achieved any great size and was always second to Glasgow in its number of Jewish residents.

RESOURCES

Synagogue

Edinburgh Hebrew Congregation. 4 Salisbury Road.
Tel: 0131-667-3144.

Kosher Food

Information. Tel: 0131-667-1521.

CHAPTER NINE

Ireland

*I*F AMERICAN JEWS know anything at all about their Irish brethren it is that at some point Dublin had a Jewish mayor. 'Tis true. Robert Briscoe was Lord Mayor of Dublin from 1956 to 1957 and again from 1961 to 1962. But Irish Jewish history begins long before that—in the twelfth and thirteenth centuries—though the community has never been a large one.

A group of five Jews first petitioned for admission to Ireland in 1079, according to the *Annals of Inisfallen* (an Ireland-centric history of the world up until the time of St. Patrick dating from the early-eleventh century), but they were unsuccessful. Later, in the twelfth and thirteenth centuries, we can infer that a small group of merchants lived and did business there because the Exchequer of the Jews (see chapter 1) maintained a presence in

Ireland. But that ended in 1290 when all Jews were expelled from Britain.

Resettlement in Ireland began, as it did in England, with refugees from the Inquisition in Spain and Portugal at the end of the fifteenth century, and records show that in the mid-sixteenth century, the mayor of Cork might have been Jewish or of Jewish origin. Later in the century, Trinity College, founded in Dublin in 1591, offered Hebrew studies.

By 1661 there was a Sephardic synagogue in Dublin in Crane Lane. Its founders were probably Conversos from Holland who came to Ireland as Protestant export merchants. The appointment of Isaac Pereira as King William III's commissary-general for his expeditionary army to Ireland brought a few more Jews to Dublin.

A few Polish and German Jewish families joined the community in the early part of the eighteenth century, but it wasn't until the latter part that more Central and Eastern European Jews joined them and there were roughly forty families. At the time the small community was comprised mostly of jewelers.

Although Dublin was home to most of Ireland's Jews, there was a congregation in Cork from 1725 to 1796, and another that dated from about 1860. The earlier congregation was made up of people in the import business—purveyors of wine and other goods from Spain and Portugal. But Jews ventured outside of Dublin even before this time, when one became a resident of Waterford in 1702.

The presence of a small number of Jews in Catholic Ireland created a good deal of missionary activity during the eighteenth century, and it was successful in gaining converts. One man, Abraham Jacobs, was baptized and later translated the Anglican *Book of Common Prayer* into Hebrew. Indeed, the Jewish population had been diminished so much by the combination of conversion and dispersal to other places that the community could no longer afford to keep up the synagogue, which closed in 1791. It had never been a prosperous or particularly strong community—its cemetery was financed with money lent from a London Jewish group and even its Torah was borrowed.

Although there was no anti-Jewish violence in Ireland during this early period, one cannot infer from this that the Irish were thrilled about having Jews in their midst. Legislation designed to make citizens of foreign Jews was rejected over and over, and other bills (1780, 1783) that granted other aliens the right to become citizens specifically denied the same rights to Jews. The 1783 Irish Naturalization Act was repealed in 1816, and by that time only three Jewish families were left in Dublin.

Some six years later, in 1822, Jews from Germany, Poland, and England began to arrive in Dublin and the nucleus of a new community was formed. In the last decades of the nineteenth century there were 450 Jews in Ireland. Refugees from Russia would join them and by 1901, the Jewish population of Ireland was 3,769. Although the majority lived in Dublin and were employed in the small trades and in money lending, there were also communities in Cork, Limerick, and Waterford in what is now the Irish Republic, and in Belfast and Londonderry in what is now Northern Ireland.

The kind of anti-Jewish violence that was an all-too-familiar fact of Jewish life in continental Europe for so many centuries didn't occur in Ireland. However, there were some anti-Jewish riots in Limerick in 1884 and in Cork in 1894. But a bigger such problem arose in Limerick in 1904. There, a local priest who had probably been influenced by anti-Semitism during the Dreyfus Affair while he was on a trip to France, began attacking Jews from the pulpit. The attacks focused on Jews as usurers, and as a result Jewish businesses were boycotted for two years. The loss of livelihood forced some 75 percent of the Jewish residents to leave, and what had been a community of 200 at the start of the boycott had dwindled to fewer than 40 by the end. The hateful priest was finally forced out and the Limerick community reestablished itself during World War I.

The Jewish community has never officially taken sides in the conflict between Ireland and England, but in practice Jews have been sympathetic to the Irish nationalist cause. During the 1916 Easter Rebellion, any number of Jewish homes in Dublin sheltered the rebels. Robert Briscoe, Dublin's first Jewish mayor, was himself a member of the Irish Republican Army and it was on the rebels' behalf that he went to the United States in 1917 to raise money from Irish-Americans. Ireland's first Chief Rabbi, Isaac Herzog, was a friend of Eamon de Valera, Ireland's first president, and Dublin solicitor Michael Noyk defended members of the Irish Republican Sinn Fein Party and was friends with Michael Collins, the Irish Republican nationalist.

In 1921 the southern part of Ireland became free of English rule. For the Jews of the new Irish Free State—later the Republic of Ireland—this meant that they were no longer under the aegis of England's chief rabbinate or its institutions. They now had their own Chief Rabbi, Isaac Herzog, and their own representative council. Jews in Northern Ireland continued to follow England's Chief Rabbi. In 1937, Judaism was recognized by the Irish constitution as a minority faith and Jews were assured freedom from discrimination.

The Second World War brought some new difficulties. Although Ireland was officially neutral, Irish anti-British sympathy led some to support Germany—as if to say, the enemy of my enemy is my friend. That, coupled with immigration restrictions, made for a troublesome situation for the Irish Jewish community. Other tensions would surface later when pressure from the Vatican prevented the Republic of Ireland from officially recognizing the new State of Israel until the 1970s, although there was unofficial recognition in 1949. In addition, members of the IRA were among terrorists trained by Israel's sworn enemies, Syria and Libya.

By the late-1960s, Ireland's Jews numbered 4,000 and were served by seven synagogues. Just to put things in perspective, the total population of the Republic was at the time 2.8 million—95 percent of whom were Roman Catholic.

In the 1980s and 1990s, the Jewish population of Ireland continued to decline. According to the census it was 2,633 in 1917; 2,127 in 1981; and by the year 2000, it was down to 1,200. Despite this decrease, the Jewish citizens of Ireland play an active role in the political life of the country out of proportion to their numbers. Labor Party member Mervyn Taylor was Ireland's first Jewish cabinet minister; Ben Briscoe, the son of Dublin's first Jewish mayor Robert Briscoe, became Lord Mayor himself in 1988; and Alan Shatter served as the Fein Gael party's environmental spokesperson.

Some anti-Semitism exists, kept alive by a tiny Irish National Socialist Party, but it tends to stay in the background and emerge only in a crisis. Stratford College, the community's main school, was set on fire in 1983 and has since been rebuilt. Although social relations between Jews and Catholics are good, the attitude toward intermarriage on the part of Catholics is, as one would expect, mostly negative. But that tends to be the attitude of Jews as well.

In the 1980s and 1990s, a number of Jewish buildings were sold by the community and are now used for other purposes. The Greenville Hall Synagogue (sold in 1986), however, has kept the original perimeter walls, windows, and cupola. The Mikvah was restored in 1984. The trend seems to be toward the consolidation of buildings and resources as the community continues to decline. The most recent casualty of the shrinking size of the community was the sale of the Adelaide Road Synagogue.

Dublin

SIGHTS

Irish Jewish Museum. 3-4 Walworth Road (off Victoria
Street), Portobello. Tel: 01-453-1797. Curator: Raphael
Siev. Hours: May–September, 11 AM–3:30 PM, Sunday,
Tuesday, Thursday. October–April, 10:30 AM–2:30 PM,
Sunday only.

Founded in 1985 by Chaim Herzog (who lived nearby), the
late, Irish-born former President of Israel, the museum,
located in a former synagogue, contains a significant
collection of items about the history of Jews in Ireland and
memorabilia of its communities. The furnishings of the
original synagogue are also here.

Old Cemetery. Ballybough. Tel: 01-836-9756. Visits
by appointment with caretaker.

RESOURCES

Jewish Community Office: Herzog House. Zion Road,
Dublin 6. Tel: 01-492-3751; Fax: 492-4680. General
information on synagogues and kosher food.

Limerick

ALTHOUGH THERE IS NO Jewish community in Limerick, the early-twentieth-century cemetery was restored in 1990 by the Limerick Civic Trust. Inquire at Jewish Community Office in Dublin (see above).

Cork

CORK IS THE ONLY other Jewish community in the Irish Republic. It maintains a cemetery and synagogue, but services are only held during Rosh Hashanah and Yom Kippur and even then, most of the minyan has to be trucked in from Dublin.

SIGHTS AND RESOURCES

Cork Hebrew Congregation. 10 South Terrace. Inquiries should be made to F. Rosehill, tel: 021-870413; fax: 270010; E-mail: rosehill@iol.ie.

Northern Ireland

THE SIX COUNTIES that make up Northern Ireland have never had too many Jews, and those that do live here are in Belfast. Londonderry had a very small community from the 1880s until the Second World War, but no longer. The community's religious authority is the Chief Rabbi of England. The population has been steadily declining.

There was probably some small group of Jews in Belfast in the late-seventeenth century when records indicate the presence of a "Jew Butcher."

A Belfast congregation was formed in 1851, made up of Jews who had settled there some ten years earlier. The Russian pogroms of the late-nineteenth century brought some Jews to Belfast and increased the community's size enough so that a school was established in 1898. By 1904 there were two synagogues. And Belfast, too, had a Jewish Lord Mayor—Sir Otto Jaffe.

Where some 1,200 Jews lived in Belfast in the early 1960s, by the late 1990s it totaled about 200. This has been due in no small measure to the ongoing political situation (known as "The Troubles") and most Belfast Jews have emigrated to Israel, the U.S., England, or Australia. Although tiny, the community maintains its share of organizations and is quite active.

Unfortunately, the Jewish burial ground in the Belfast City Cemetery on Falls Road in West Belfast is in terrible condition—it has been badly neglected, and has been the target of vandalism. A granite obelisk, erected in memory of the former Lord Mayor, Sir Otto Jaffe, by his son Daniel Joseph Jaffe, is covered in paint and graffiti.[11]

BELFAST RESOURCES

Synagogue: Belfast Hebrew Congregation and Community Center. 49 Somerset Road.
Tel: 028-90-77-9491 and 90-77-7974.
The **Community Center** has a kosher restaurant.
Call for hours.

CHAPTER TEN

Assorted Sights of Jewish Interest

WITH THE EXCEPTION OF the one on London, many of this book's chapters are quite short. It is ironic and a bit sad that the long history of the Jewish people in Britain has resulted in relatively few places for the traveler to visit. Unlike many other attractions, the ones of a specifically Jewish nature do not jump out at you. Frequently, the determined traveler has to seek them out. But those who do will be pleasantly surprised and richly rewarded. These rewards are due in no small measure to a dedicated group of people who have seen to it that a lot of what is of Jewish interest in Britain is accessible and will be preserved. Among them are Dr. Sharman Kadish of the Survey of the Jewish Built Heritage; David Jacobs of Reform Synagogues of Great Britain; Mrs. Evelyn Friedlander of the Hidden Legacy Foundation, whose work on the Jews of Devon and Cornwall is invaluable; Tony Kushner of the University of Southampton; and Charles Tucker, the archivist of the United Synagogue.

Bristol

THE JACOB'S WELL MIKVAH is believed to date from 1140. The cemetery of the same pre-Expulsion community is underneath the Queen Elizabeth Hospital School, and there is some evidence to indicate that the crypt of St. Peter's Church on St. Peter's Street was the synagogue.

Buckinghamshire

WADDESDON MANOR, built between 1874 and 1889 in French Renaissance style, was the home of Baron Ferdinand de Rothschild. It houses a collection of eighteenth-century French and English art as well as a collection of Dutch and Flemish paintings. Today it is owned and administered by the National Trust.

Hughenden Manor was the home of Benjamin Disraeli (Lord Beaconsfield) from 1848 until his death in 1881. Disraeli, who was converted to Christianity by his father when he was a child, is buried in Hughenden Church.

Cambridge

JEWISH SETTLEMENT IN this history-filled town pre-dates the celebrated university. In the late-eleventh century, Jews from Rouen, France, settled here and by the thirteenth century they had established a synagogue in Market Square. Most of Cambridge's Jews were deported to nearby Norwich by Queen Eleanor in 1275. A few remained, however, until the Expulsion fifteen years later.

The modern community dates back to 1847 and the present synagogue in Ellis Court was built in 1940. It serves the transient student community.

The medieval Jewish community owned several pieces of land—the site of Peterhouse College, the land on which part of the Divinity school now stands (St. John's Street, All Souls Passage, Bridge Street), and the site of Guild Hall.

Cambridge University has some wonderful Judaica collections including the **Schechter-Taylor Geniza** collection, the **Aldis-Wright Hebraica** collection at Trinity College, and the **Mary Frere Hebrew** collection at Girton College. With the exception of the Schechter-Taylor collection, for which visits can be arranged, these are available only to scholars.

Canterbury

THE COUNTY HOTEL: "The cellar contains the remnants of a house that had belonged to Jacob the Jew. . . . Behind his house once stood the synagogue, and the road at the back of the hotel still bears the name Jewry Lane."[12]

Chatham

THERE ARE ONLY about fifty Jews in this Kent seaport. The community dates back to the eighteenth century and was made up of small merchants who did business with the navy.

SIGHTS

Chatham Memorial Synagogue, 366 High Street, Rochester. Inquiries: Dr. C. Harris, Sutton Place, Sutton Road, Maidstone, Kent ME15 9DU. Tel: 01622-753040.

> The synagogue, built in 1869 in memory of Captain Lazarus Simon Magnus, stands on the site of a 1740 synagogue. The cemetery, in back, dates back to 1790.

Hereford

ON THE BANKS of the lovely River Wye, Hereford Cathedral sits on a site that has been sacred to the English since the days of the Saxons. The town of Hereford's cathedral dates from Norman times and is one of the best examples of that period's architecture.

Hereford Cathedral. 5 College Cloisters. Tel: 01432-359-880. Hours: Summer: Monday–Sunday, 10:00 AM–4:15 PM (last admission); Sunday, 11:00 AM–3:15

PM. Winter: Monday–Saturday 11:00 AM–3:15 PM (last admission); Closed Sunday. Admissions: £4.00, adults; £3.00, seniors, children; £10.00, family; children under 5, free.

Among the statues around the arch of the inner north porch of the cathedral, which date from circa 1280, is a small figure, the second from the bottom on the far left, that appears to be a blindfolded female with a staff in her left hand and an open book in her right. The statue is very weathered, so interpretation is difficult, but it is believed that this is a representation of Synagoga, a figure that appears in churches primarily in France and Germany. Synagoga is usually paired with a statue called Ecclesia and the two together represent the conflict between Judaism and Christianity. Where Synagoga is a blindfolded, disheveled woman with either a broken staff or staff-cum-serpent in her hand, Ecclesia is beautiful, well dressed, and adorned with a crown or a sun.

Another figure, labeled Synagogue, is in one of the stained-glass windows at the top of the left-hand light in the east window of the choir. It dates from 1871.

Leicester

THE JEWRY WALL was part of the city's Roman baths. It is one of the largest surviving Roman buildings in Britain. The derivation of the name is uncertain. And here is an interesting bit of historical trivia: In January 2001, the city of Leicester finally got around to formally removing its 800-year-old ban on Jews. Promulgated by Simon de Montfort, Earl of

Leicester, regarded as the father of the English Parliament (see chapter 1) the 1231 edict barred Jews from living in the city. Leicester's City Council unanimously rejected the de Montfort edict in advance of Britain's Holocaust Memorial Day. Indeed it was about time.

> **Leicester's Synagogue** (Highfield Street. Tel: 0116-2706622) was built in 1897.

Oxford

*T*HE JEWISH POPULATION of Oxford dates back to the early-twelfth century and there are records indicating the presence of a synagogue in 1227 that was founded by descendents of Jews who accompanied William the Conqueror to England in 1066. Prior to the Expulsion, this was one of England's most important Jewish communities.

The medieval community lived on **Great Jewry Street**—today's St. Aldate's Street. Moyse's, Lombard's, and Jacob's Halls were once Jewish residences. The medieval cemetery was located where the Botanical Garden is now—opposite Magdalen College.

Isaac Abendana was one of the few practicing Jews (the others had converted to Christianity) to be allowed to teach at Oxford (Magdalen College) in the period of the Resettlement.

The present community was organized in 1842 and it remained very small until World War II when Jews escaping German bombs in places such as London increased the population.

The **Synagogue,** 21 Richmond Road, was built in the 1970s.

The **Bodleian Library** has some 30,000 Hebrew books and

about 3,500 Hebrew manuscripts, one from Egypt in the fifth century BCE. These are not open to the public.

The **Ashmolean Museum** (Beaumont Street. Tel: 01865-278000. Hours: Tuesday–Saturday, 10 AM–5 PM; Sunday 2 PM–5 PM) has some antiquities from Jerusalem and some fragments of the Dead Sea Scrolls. It also contains the Bodleian Bowl, which belonged to Rabbi Yehiel, of Paris. Rabbi Yehiel, a noted thirteenth century scholar was leader of Paris's Jewish community.

Ramsgate

EAST CLIFF LODGE is what remains of the residence of Sir Moses and Lady Judith Montefiore. They are buried in a nearby mausoleum on Honeysuckle Road modeled after Rachel's Tomb (located between Jerusalem and Bethlehem) next to the synagogue that they built in 1833. The synagogue was designed and constructed by David Mocatta.

Rochester

THIS SEAPORT NO longer has a Jewish community but it did in the Middle Ages. Rochester Cathedral is notable for, among other things, one of the few examples of Ecclesia and Synagoga in England.

SIGHTS

Rochester Cathedral

At the entrance to the cathedral chapter house are statues of
Ecclesia and Synagoga. These date back to medieval times
and represent the conflict of Church and Synagogue.
Synagoga is sad, her staff and the tablets of the Ten
Commandments are broken. (See page 105.)

Southrop

*I*N THE **Church of St. Peter**, there is a statue of Moses
holding the Tablets of the Law. On one side of Moses
stands a statue of Synagoga and on his other is Ecclesia. Ecclesia
(the Church) has her back turned to Synagoga. Not many of the
medieval Ecclesia and Synagoga representations survive in
Britain. It is believed, though, that these allegorical figures were
less prevalent here than in continental Europe. (See page 105.)

Endnotes

1. D'Blossiers Tovey, LL.D, *Anglia Judaica* or *A History of the Jews in England.* First published in 1738; translated into modern English and republished in 1990 by Weidenfeld and Nicholson, London.

2. Antonia Fraser, *Cromwell: Our Chief of Men.* Weidenfeld and Nicholson, London, 1974.

3. Quoted in *The Jews of Britain: A Thousand Years of History,* by Pamela Fletcher Jones. The Windrush Press, Gloucestershire, 1990.

4. *Encyclopedia Judaica,* Keter Publishing, Jerusalem, 1997.

5. Ibid.

6. Dr. Sharman Kadish, The Survey of the Jewish Built Heritage, Manchester, England, 2001.

7. The Imperial War Museum.

8. Dr. Sharman Kadish, The Survey of the Jewish Built Heritage, Manchester, England, 2001.

9. *Encyclopedia Judaica.*

10. Dr. Sharman Kadish, The Survey of the Jewish Built Heritage, Manchester, England, 2001.

11. Ibid.

12. *The Jewish Yearbook,* Vallentine Mitchell, London, 1999.

Suggested Reading

Geoffrey Alderman, *Modern British Jewry*, Clarendon Press, 1998.

David Englander, ed., *A Documentary History of Jewish Immigrants in Britain 1840–1920*, Leicester University Press, 1994.

Israel Finestein, *Anglo-Jewry in Changing Times*, Vallentine Mitchell, 1999.

Sharman Kadish (editor), *Building Jerusalem: Jewish Architecture in Britain*, Vallentine Mitchell, 1996.

Paul Lindsay, *The Synagogues of London*, Vallentine Mitchell, 1993.

Robin Mundill, *England's Jewish Solution 1262–1290*, Cambridge University Press, 1998.

Aubrey Newman, *The Board of Deputies of British Jews*, Vallentine Mitchell, 1987.

W. D. Rubenstein, *A History of Jews in the English-Speaking World*, Palgrave, 1995.

Websites

The Survey of the Jewish Built Heritage, http://www.art.man.ac.uk/reltheol/jewish/heritage/home.htm

The International Survey of Jewish Monuments, http://www.best.com~isjm

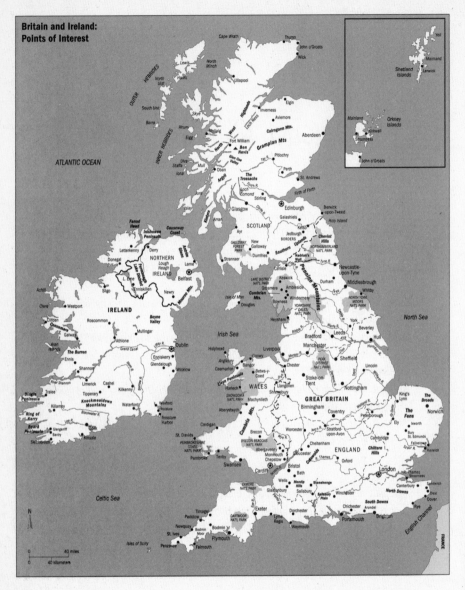

**Britain and Ireland:
Points of Interest**

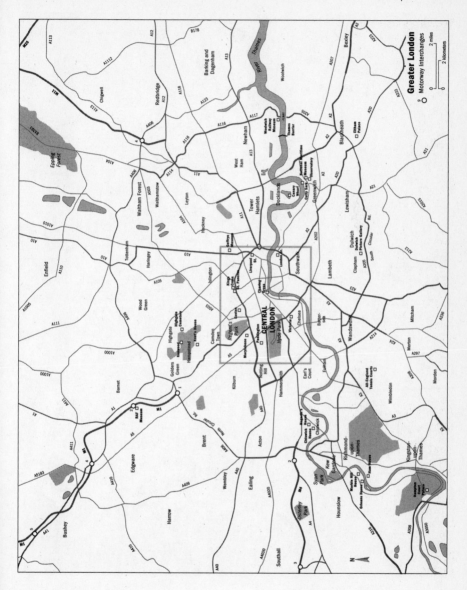

Greater London

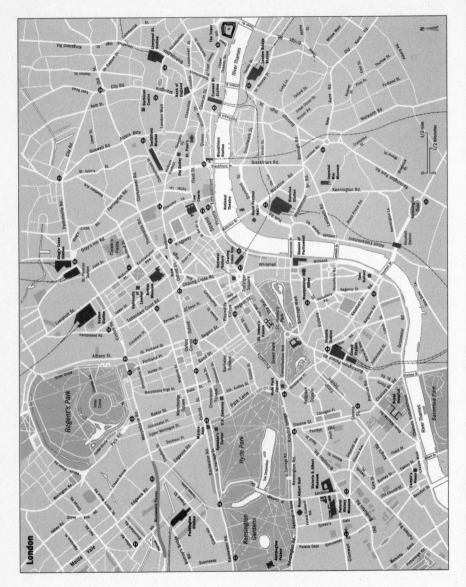

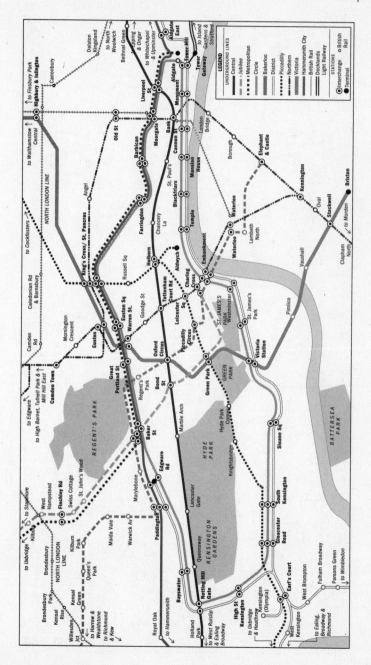

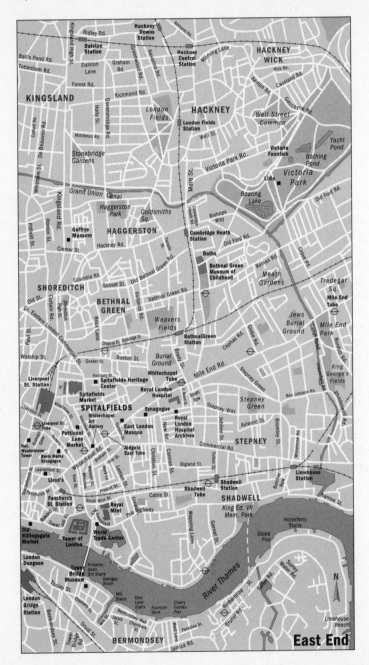

East End

Index

About the Author

Toni L. Kamins has Jewish travel in her genes; for hundreds of years there have been rabbis in her family, and family legend has it that she is descended from Rabbi Judah Loew of Prague, the sixteenth-century creator of the Golem. Toni teaches basic Hebrew and Judaism at her local synagogue and is an active member of the congregation. A freelance journalist and former editor, she has covered an array of Jewish and secular subjects for *The New York Times,* the *New York Daily News, The Jerusalem Post, New York* magazine, *The Village Voice, Forward,* and other publications as well as Web sites devoted to travel topics. Toni also edited and contributed to various major travel guides and wrote articles on the Middle East and on the Shoah for the book *Our Times: An Illustrated History of the 20th Century* (Turner Publishing).

She resides in New York City with her husband. Her e-mail address is toni@completejewishguides.com.